SECRET
PEAK DISTRICT

Mike Smith

AMBERLEY

About the Author

Mike Smith lives with his wife Jo-Ann in the ancient Peak District market town of Chapel-en-le-Frith, where he is a long-serving parish councillor. He is a former headteacher of Silverdale School, Sheffield, and he is the author of a number of topographical books and guide books covering various regions of England and France. For fourteen years he has contributed monthly features to *Derbyshire Life and Countryside* magazine.

First published 2017

Amberley Publishing
The Hill, Stroud
Gloucestershire, GL5 4EP

www.amberley-books.com

ISBN 978 1 4456 6248 0 (print)
ISBN 978 1 4456 6249 7 (ebook)

British Library Cataloguing in Publication Data.
A catalogue record for this book is available from the British Library.

Origination by Amberley Publishing.
Printed in Great Britain.

Contents

Introduction

The Peak District is a land of high moors and narrow gorges, dark gritstone edges and white limestone cliffs, bleak plateaux and lush valleys, fine churches and grand country houses, stone-built villages and spa towns. In 1951, much of the region was designated as Britain's first national park and it is now one of the most visited national parks in the world, second only to the Mount Kyoto National Park in Japan.

Because the Peak District is familiar to millions of visitors, it might be thought that it contains few secrets, but this is far from the case. Some of the region's most charming villages and country estates are not as well known as they might be because they are situated well away from the normal tourist trails. One of the area's most beautiful valleys has a fascinating secret history that embraces long-lost industries and the lives and times of a remarkable family that was the dominant presence in the valley for exactly 100 years.

Although some of the larger settlements in the Peak District are very well known, they contain much that is hidden. Bakewell has many secret ingredients other than those found in its famous pudding, not least those that are revealed in its numerous arcades and alleyways. Some of the celebrated wood carvings made by several generations of the Hunstone family for the 'Cathedral of the Peak', the Church of St John the Baptist in Tideswell, are tantalisingly hard to spot unless you know exactly where to look for them.

When viewed from the summit of gardens known as the Slopes, the townscape of the famous spa area of Buxton is one of the finest in England, but the spectacular domes that are such visible features of the skyline are really the outer skins of some truly wonderful hidden ceilings. Ashbourne is a town with lots of fine Georgian and Victorian buildings, but the façades of several of these buildings are masks that conceal the evidence of much earlier Tudor origins. And away from the towns of the region, there are several highly unusual buildings whose contrasting façades indicate split personalities.

The Peak District countryside contains innumerable reminders of times past. There are mysterious Neolithic and Bronze Age stone circles and structures left over from the centuries when lead was the Peak District's 'gold'. The roads across the Pennines are dotted with toll houses that have survived from the coaching days and the landscape is scored with tracks that are the fossilised remains of some of the country's earliest railways.

Many of the Peak District's secrets were revealed to me during fourteen years of researching and writing monthly features for *Derbyshire Life and Countryside* magazine. One of the most surprising of these secrets is described in the chapter entitled 'Grand Illusions', which discloses that much of the spectacular scenery of the Peak District depends on the existence of illusions of grand scale, even in places where the real dimensions of the landscape are actually quite modest. Indeed, this remarkable contrast between apparent scale and real scale is one of the main reasons why this area of upland England is so special.

Part One

The Secrets of Peak District Towns

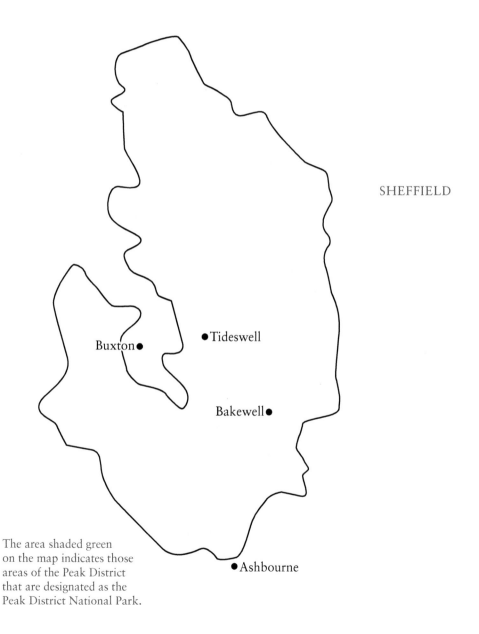

SHEFFIELD

●Tideswell

Buxton●

Bakewell●

●Ashbourne

The area shaded green
on the map indicates those
areas of the Peak District
that are designated as the
Peak District National Park.

1. Buxton Undercover

Buxton sits in an upland valley at the heart of the Peak District, where the high gritstone moors of the Dark Peak meet the limestone plateau of the White Peak. Seen from the summit of the steep landscaped gardens known as the Slopes, the townscape of the famous Derbyshire spa is one of the finest in England. It embraces spectacular domes, shapely cupolas, elegant crescents and a grand hotel.

What a bird's-eye view does not reveal is the equally wonderful quality of the architecture hidden immediately below the roofs of these edifices. On your next visit to Buxton, I urge you to go 'undercover' by walking into the grandest buildings of the town and then looking upwards. By doing so you will discover a Buxton of spectacular ceilings, some of which had remained hidden for many years.

To learn why a town in an area otherwise characterised by simple stone cottages and farmsteads should have such pretentious architecture, it is necessary to trace the history of the settlement back to Roman times. It was the Romans who discovered the health benefits of the waters that flow from the limestone hills to the south of Buxton, before

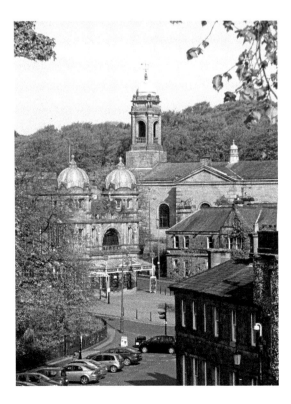

Buxton from the summit of the Slopes.

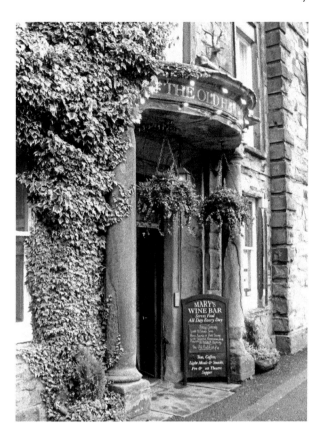

Old Hall Hotel.

emerging as thermal springs in the town, which the Romans called Aquae Arnemetiae (Spa of the Goddess of the Grove).

After the Romans left, the people who lived in the area around Buxton continued to believe in the restorative properties of the springs, but the town only came to prominence again as a spa when Mary Queen of Scots paid a number of visits to 'take the waters' as a cure for her rheumatism. At the time, the captive queen was in the custodianship of the Earl of Shrewsbury, the third husband of Bess of Hardwick, a redoubtable woman who became the richest woman in England as a result of a succession of well-made marriages.

DID YOU KNOW?

In June 1975, snow famously stopped play in a county cricket match held in Buxton. The match between Derbyshire and Lancashire was umpired by Dickie Bird, who recalls: 'When I went out to inspect the wicket, the snow came to the top of my boots. I had never seen anything like it.' Dickie had every right to be surprised because snow had not fallen so late in the year since 1888.

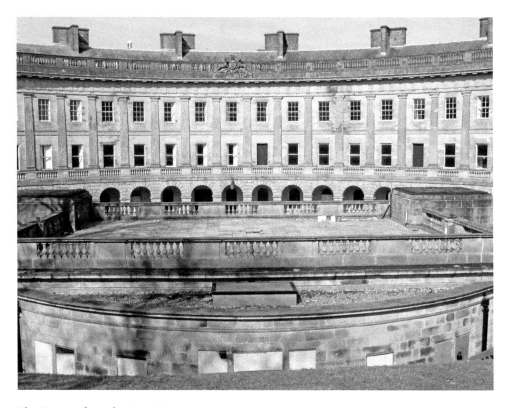

The Crescent from the Pump Room.

During her visits to Buxton, the equally formidable Mary stayed at the Old Hall Hotel, which had been commissioned by the Earl and Countess of Shrewsbury in 1573. The queen left her mark on the building in the form of an etching that she is said to have scratched with a diamond ring onto a windowpane in the room where she slept. The restored etching reads: 'Buxton, whose warm waters have made thy name famous, perchance I shall visit thee no more – Farewell.'

However, Buxton did not fully take off as a spa until the 5th Duke of Devonshire, William Cavendish, hatched a plan to convert the town into a northern Bath. He began his transformation in the late eighteenth century by using profits from his copper mine at Ecton, in the Manifold Valley, 20 miles south of Buxton. His first step was to build a fashionable crescent to rival the famous crescents in Bath. To design the building, the duke commissioned John Carr, the York architect, who had come to his attention because of his work at Wentworth Woodhouse, an enormous country house near Rotherham.

Although Carr's Crescent occupies a sunken position at the foot of the Slopes, it sits centre stage in the spa. Pilasters and a balustrade decorate its precise geometry, and rusticated ground-floor arcades give the building a continental touch. In the Derbyshire volume of his *Buildings of England*, Nikolaus Pevsner describes the building as being more elegant than John Wood's Royal Crescent at Bath. The duke, whose coat of arms is carved in the rooftop balustrade, must have been very pleased with this first step in his ambitious scheme.

In its early days, the Crescent provided a house for the duke, a hotel, lodging rooms, card and billiard rooms and an Assembly Room, where balls and other fashionable gatherings could take place. Having outdone Wood with his exterior design, Carr took the work of the great Robert Adam as the model for the interior of the Assembly Room, not least in the decoration of the blue and gold ceiling, supported by gilt-topped Corinthian columns and pilasters.

For much of the twentieth century this beautiful ceiling could be admired for free by people using Buxton Library, which utilised the former Assembly Room as a reading room. However, the great ceiling was hidden from public view for over two decades after the building was closed in 1992, following the discovery of acute structural problems. During this sad and shameful period of neglect, Carr's masterpiece became the 'most at-risk grade I-listed building in England'.

At the time of writing, a £46-million restoration project has finally been given the go-ahead. The aim is to transform the Crescent into a seventy-nine-bed hotel, supplemented by boutique shops and a restaurant. A new rear extension will accommodate indoor and outdoor pools, kitchens and a plant room, and the adjacent natural baths will be reborn as a thermal spa. The Pump Room, situated opposite the Crescent, will reopen and that wonderful ceiling in the former Assembly Room will be restored to its full glory.

The privilege of seeing the renovated ceiling will not only be confined to guests staying at the new spa hotel, because the Buxton Crescent and Thermal Spa Heritage Trust will ensure that there will be public access to the Assembly Room on at least sixty days per year.

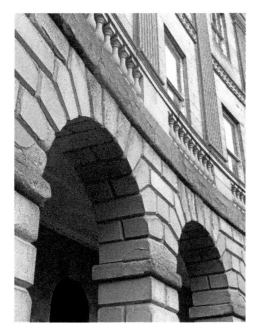 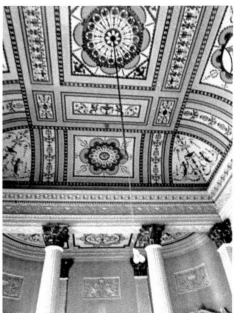

Above left: Detail of arcading in the Crescent.

Above right: Ceiling of the Assembly Room.

DID YOU KNOW?

Although Buxton is known for its high rainfall and extreme winter weather, it has always attracted many visitors. The 1936 edition of the *Buxton Guidebook*, which describes the town as 'the spa of the Blue Waters', contains the following description: 'At an altitude of 1,000 feet, with a consequent tonic and invigorating climate, Buxton has air of unsurpassed purity and dryness.'

The second phase of the 5th Duke's plan, also delegated to John Carr, was to build a huge stable block to house the horses, which would be used to bring the expected influx of visitors to Buxton. Carr designed the stables in an elegant Georgian style and arranged them around the circumference of an enormous exercise yard.

However, the arrival of the railways in the 1860s meant that there was no longer a need for such a large stable block. Persuaded by his land agent, Mr Wilmot, the 6th Duke agreed to fund a scheme to convert the stables into a hospital for the 'sick poor'. This novel plan went ahead despite the objections of Dr Robertson, a prominent local doctor, who said that 'no human creatures could be healthy where horses had lived.'

The conversion plan reached new heights of extravagant practicality in 1880 when the exercise area of half an acre was covered in spectacular fashion by the erection of a dome,

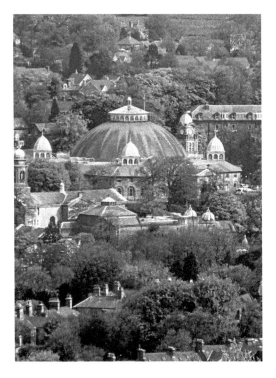

The Devonshire Dome.

which for many years was the largest unsupported dome in the world – larger than the domes of St Paul's Cathedral, the Duomo in Florence, and even St Peter's in Rome.

The design of the dome was the work of Robert Rippon Duke. Although the Buxton architect had been confident that he could create a roof of these unprecedented proportions, he became alarmed during its construction when he heard the news about the collapse of the Tay Bridge, which had been based on a similar iron-girder construction. Duke rushed to the building site and ordered an immediate check on the condition of every rivet in the dome.

In 2006, when the NHS decided that the Devonshire Royal was no longer viable as a hospital, the University of Derby's vice chancellor, Professor Roger Waterhouse, put in a bid for the building to be a new home for the High Peak College, which had merged with the university in 1998. Professor Waterhouse's bold vision became a reality in 2006 when the new Buxton Campus of the University of Derby was opened by Prince Charles. If the University of Oxford has the distinction of being located in a 'city of dreaming spires', the University of Derby would now have a campus in a 'town of dreaming domes'.

The coffee bar and restaurant facilities of the Devonshire Dome are open to members of the general public, who are greeted by an awesome view of the interior of the vast dome. The ceiling has a span of 44 metres and is supported by twenty-two steel ribs that rise dramatically from a circular colonnade of forty-four pillars.

Robert Rippon Duke had been given the confidence to design a dome to cover the exercise yard of the Stables by the success of his design for the large concert hall that was added to the Victorian Pavilion Gardens complex in the 1870s. The spectacular octagonal roof of the concert hall is supported by a huge metal ring beam, which was subjected to a rather poorly executed renovation in the 1950s. Recent technological advances have allowed the local authority to conduct an invasive condition survey of the structure. When

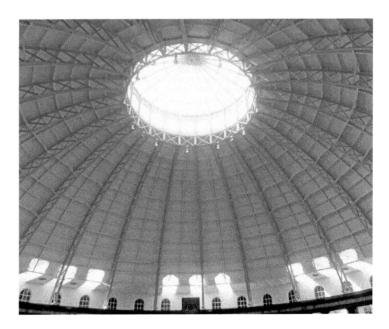

Interior of the
Devonshire Dome.

this investigation identified the urgent need for significant repair work, the authority embarked on a renovation that should save this wonderful ceiling for years to come.

The remainder of the Pavilion Gardens complex comprises a modern indoor swimming pool, added in 1972, and a long glass and iron building, designed in 1872 by Edward Milner, who was clearly inspired by the revolutionary design of London's Crystal Palace, built for the Great Exhibition of 1851.

A section of the Pavilion Gardens was badly damaged by a fire in 1982. However, the inferno turned out to be a blessing in disguise because the subsequent repair involved the removal of a false roof that had completely hidden the original ceiling, which had an

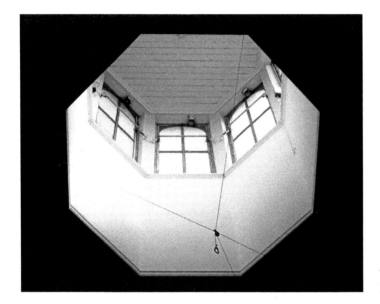

The Lantern in the Pavilion Gardens.

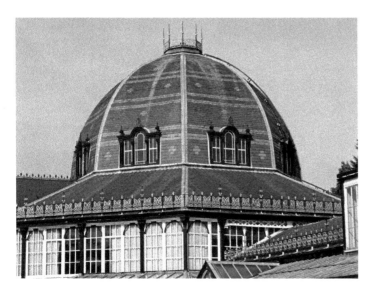

Octagonal roof of the Concert Hall.

octagonal rooftop lantern as its centrepiece. As well as exposing the internal structure of the lantern, the opening up of the space underneath it enabled a second tier to be added to the Pavilion's coffee lounge and restaurant.

The long range of the Pavilion Gardens terminates in a delightful Edwardian Opera House, designed by Frank Matcham, the prolific theatre architect. The building was carefully renovated in 1979 after being used for some years as a cinema. The restored auditorium is covered by a truly stunning ceiling that is a restrained riot of Rococo-style decoration. The Opera House is now the focal point of the Buxton Festival, which has grown year by year and is now an annual extravaganza of opera productions, concert performances, recitals and literary events. Of course, when audiences wait for performances to begin in the Opera House, they have the added bonus of being able to stare at the glorious ceiling, which has a mesmeric effect on all those present.

Another fine example of 'undercover Buxton' is to be found in the former Thermal Baths building adjacent to the Crescent. Constructed in 1853, the building comprised sixteen private baths for ladies and twelve for gentleman. Writing at the beginning of the twentieth century, Dr Thresh attempted a scientific explanation of the supposed power of the waters to wash away gout, rheumatism, neuralgia, skin disorders and heart diseases. He said:

> The presence of nitrogen and carbonic acid, in their nascent state, and the recent demonstration by Lord Rayleigh of the presence of argon and helium, and by Lord Blythswood of radium, may explain the action of these waters. The molecular activity of

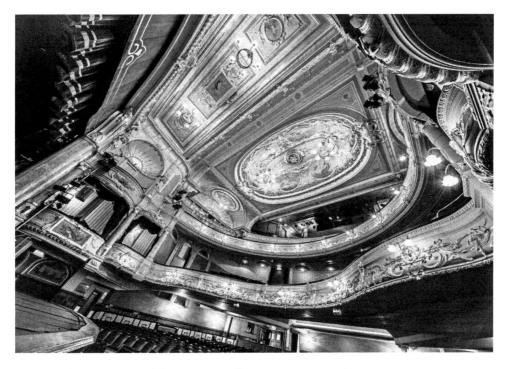

Ceiling of the Opera House. (Photo courtesy of Buxton Opera House)

radium is the most powerful of any known body, and it is probable that, in combination with the above gases, it sets up a corresponding activity in the peripheral nerve endings of the tissues of the skin which is thence communicated throughout the whole system.

It is not surprising to learn that doctors and their patients would become increasingly sceptical about such outlandish claims for the health-giving properties of thermal and natural spring waters. Although faith in water treatments remained high in many continental countries, their use went into gradual decline in this country. In 1987 Buxton's Thermal Baths building, once so sought after as a medical facility, was converted into a shopping precinct called the Cavendish Arcade, now home to several very stylish boutiques.

As well as preserving and restoring the original decorated tiles of the Thermal Baths, the developers added a bold new element to the building. This takes the form of a barrel-vaulted glass canopy, decorated by the celebrated stained-glass artist Brian Clarke, whose semi-abstract composition was inspired by the sight of autumn leaves falling on the roof of the conservatory in the Pavilion Gardens. This colourful glass canopy is the latest addition to the many ceilings that are such a distinctive feature of Buxton.

DID YOU KNOW?

John Martin Robinson's *The Architecture of Northern England* paints the following portrait of Buxton: 'The splendid Italianate and Francophile buildings have the feeling of being gathered together on the side of a mountain to make a Rex Whistler capriccio, rather than form part of a real town.'

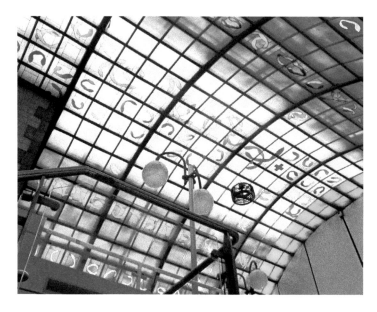

Glass canopy of the Cavendish Arcade.

2. Ashbourne's Hidden Heritage

Travellers approaching Ashbourne from the south catch their first glimpse of Pennine hills when the town comes into view. For these visitors, this old market town at the southern edge of the Peak District is their first encounter with northern England, but travellers arriving from the north have a very different perspective. When the road that has taken them through the stone-built villages of the White Peak begins its steep descent into the town, they are transported quite unexpectedly into a street of red-brick houses. For them, Ashbourne is the first settlement in lowland England.

Many of the town's buildings reflect this dual personality, combining northern qualities of sturdiness with a touch of southern picturesqueness. Unlike all the other settlements located in the Peak District countryside to the north of the town, Ashbourne is largely brick-built, but stone is still in evidence. In fact, stone and brick buildings often sit side by side in the town. They are also likely to share identical architectural features, regardless of the material used in their construction.

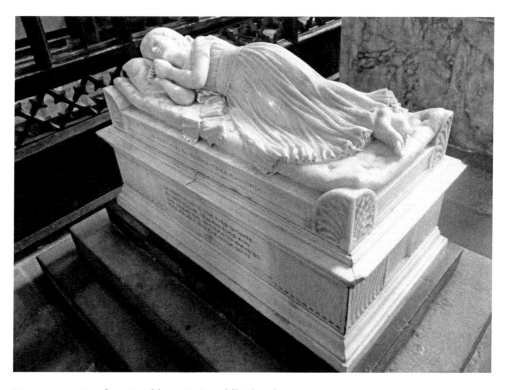

Monument to Penelope Boothby in St Oswald's Church.

The northern approach road leads directly to the triangular Market Place. In the words of Tony Grace, a director of the Ashbourne Town Partnership: 'On Market days, it would be hard to find a better entrance to the town, not only because the twice-weekly stall market is so vibrant, but also because it creates a strong sense of place, with present-day stall holders selling their goods on the same plot of land where street trading began in 1257.'

Aside from the Market Place, the streets and alleyways of this very attractive country town contain not only chain stores and supermarkets, but also lots of excellent independent shops, including some particularly fine ladies' boutiques, florists, craft shops, antique shops, small art galleries and speciality food shops, with bistros, cafés, old-world pubs and former coaching inns providing plenty of opportunities for refreshment. There is also a shuttle bus service to a retail park on the edge of the town.

With regard to visitors approaching Ashbourne from the south, they have an early view of the tall, slender spire of St Oswald's parish church. The spire, 65 metres high and pierced by twenty dormers, makes an immediate impression as a very beautiful structure, although its impact on the townscape would be even greater if the church had been built on a rather less sunken plot of land.

George Eliot described St Oswald's as 'the finest mere parish church in the kingdom'. Viewed from the churchyard, the building certainly lives up to this billing, but the interior looks a little disappointing at first sight, because the absence of a north aisle gives the nave

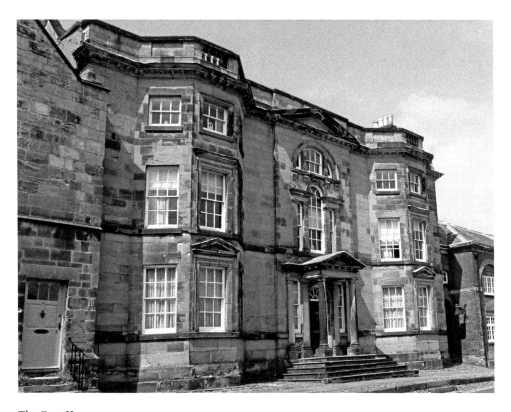

The Grey House.

a rather lopsided look. On the other hand, the transepts are so large and impressive that they could almost be mistaken for the main axis of the church. They contain an extensive collection of tombs and brasses dedicated to the memory of various prominent local families. However, it is a pity that these monuments are crowded together in a single chapel in the north transept, especially as the church's greatest treasure, a white marble sculpture of a sleeping child by Thomas Banks, almost suffocates in this congestion.

The child depicted in Banks' tenderly carved monument is Penelope Boothby, who died one month before her sixth birthday. The inscription reads: 'She was in form and intellect most exquisite. The unfortunate parents ventured all on this frail bark, and the wreck was total.' The quotation is repeated in French, Latin and Italian, for it is claimed that young Penelope had some grasp of all these languages.

The path through the churchyard climbs to wrought-iron gates that open onto Church Street, which is a mecca for collectors of antiques, who make pilgrimages to Ashbourne from far and wide. Collectable furniture, ornaments, sculptures and paintings spill out onto the pavement in front of several premises.

Directly opposite the church gates is the stone-built former grammar school, founded in 1585. The boldness and solidity of the building is softened by mullioned and transomed windows, a delicately carved coat of arms and a row of four gables flanked by two larger gables. Adjoining the old school is the very elaborate façade of a Georgian town house known as the Grey House. Two large bay windows flank the central portico and, above the pediment, there is a Venetian window topped by a large semicircular tripartite window. This surprisingly complex architectural arrangement is repeated precisely, but in brick rather than in stone, on a building known as the Mansion House, which stands on the opposite side of the road from the Grey House.

DID YOU KNOW?

Between 1737 and 1784, Dr Samuel Johnson, the famous lexicographer, was a frequent visitor to Ashbourne. His host was his friend, Dr Taylor, who lived in the Mansion House on Church Street. Dr Johnson greatly enjoyed his visits to 'Ashbourne in the Peak'. In a letter penned in 1771, he wrote, 'Let not the barren name of the Peak terrify you. I have never wanted for strawberries and cream.'

The rest of Church Street contains several impressive rows of almshouses and lots of good Georgian town houses. Church Street is often described as the best street in Derbyshire and the quality of its architecture is certainly there for all to see, but, according to retired architect Tony Short, there is much more to this street, and much more to Ashbourne generally, than meets the eye.

During his career Tony was involved in the renovation of various buildings in the town centre and came to realise that many of Ashbourne's Georgian and Victorian façades

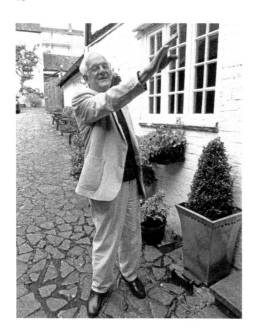

Tony Short.

conceal a much earlier architectural legacy. Since taking retirement, he has been able to devote his considerable energy and enthusiasm to the task of researching this hidden architectural heritage.

Tony offered to take me on an architectural tour of Ashbourne with a difference. Rather than admiring buildings from the outside, we would venture within them. We met in Flower Café in the Market Place, where we were lucky enough to find seats at a table large enough for Tony to unfurl a full-sized facsimile of a sixteenth-century illustrated map that has proved to be of great help in his investigations.

The original map, now held in the National Archives at Kew, was commissioned in 1546 for use as evidence in a high court dispute between Matthew Kniveton and Thomas Cockayne about the gating of a drovers' road linking Ashbourne and Kniveton. Tony said, 'This superbly drawn map is an absolutely invaluable guide to Tudor Ashbourne, because it depicts all the buildings in three dimensions and shows the configuration of every street in the town.'

As the basic layout of Ashbourne remains remarkably unchanged to this day, it is possible to match many of the buildings shown on the map with structures that have survived to the present. Knowing that his speculations about the exact age of these buildings could be converted into hard evidence by the use of dendrochronology, which involves the analysis of growth rings to date timbers, Tony turned to the expertise of Robert Howard of the Nottingham Tree Ring Dating Laboratory and obtained funding to support his research from the Vernacular Architecture Group, of which he is a member.

Having explained his methodology, Tony was ready to show me some of his findings. He began by pointing across the street to a jeweller's shop called Silvarious. Seen from the outside, this building would seem to be a most unlikely subject for an investigation into Tudor architecture. It could easily be thought that the façade, featuring large ground-floor windows with fine displays of handcrafted jewellery, is Georgian in origin at the very earliest.

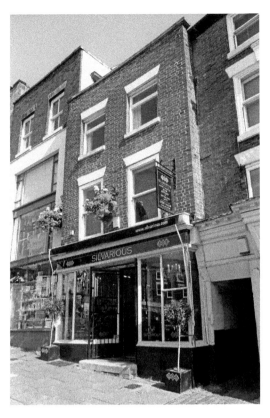 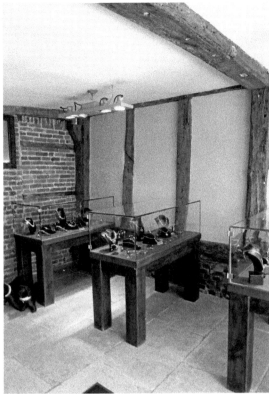

The exterior and interior of Silvarious.

Sensing my surprise at his choice, Tony ushered me into the interior. Although the display area is the very epitome of twenty-first-century designer chic, it is enclosed by ancient timber-framed walls that have been beautifully restored. Tony pointed out an exposed oak beam that must have supported an overhanging upper floor in Tudor times, with the space below this jetty being filled in at a later date to create a frontage that became continuous with the upper floors.

Silvarious' owner, Eileen O'Donnell, was responsible for stripping down the walls to expose the old timbers and the brickwork between them. Given the care she has lavished on preserving the architectural heritage of her premises and the fine quality of the jewellery displayed there, it comes as no surprise to learn that Eileen is a very successful businesswoman who has further jewellery shops in Bakewell, Derby and Matlock.

After we left the jewellers, Tony took me into an alleyway that runs alongside the building and showed me yet more surviving ancient exposed timberwork. In this case, the timbers are part of an external wall. He then took me across the road to Ashbourne's famous fish and chip shop, which is housed in a low black-and-white building with an array of mock half-timbers and a black-and-white gabled porch. Although the half-timbering on the exterior has a distinctly 'mock' look about it, the timbers in the interior of the shop have been dated by dendrochronology as genuine survivals from 1420.

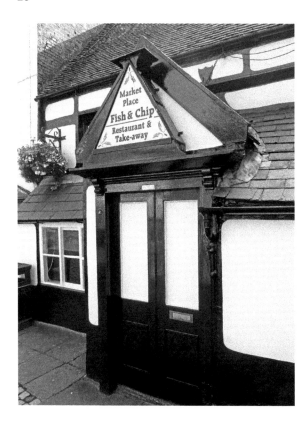

Fish and Chip shop in the
Market Place.

DID YOU KNOW?

Ashbourne's Royal Shrovetide football match is played over two days in the
shopping streets, streams and culverts of the town. The 'goalposts' are 3 miles apart,
the 'pitch' is 2 miles wide and there is no limit to the number of players. The match is
played between the 'Up'ards' (people who live on the north side of Henmore Brook)
and the 'Down'ards' (people who live on the south side), and the players inevitably
end up splashing around in the brook at some stage during the free-for-all.

Our next port of call was the Lamplight Restaurant in Victoria Square, located just
below the Market Place. The ancient building housing the restaurant has retained
its overhanging upper floor, but the old timbers on its façade have been masked by
rendering. Fortunately, as Tony revealed when he took me through an archway adjacent
to the building, ancient timber framing has been fully exposed on the side wall of the
restaurant, which flanks a fine old courtyard.

As the 1546 map indicates, courtyards were a common feature of Tudor Ashbourne.
They were cleverly created by alternating buildings that had their gables facing the

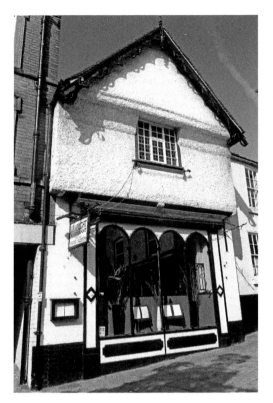 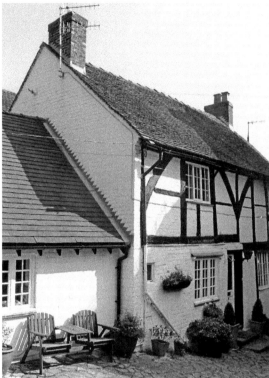

Above left: Frontage of the Lamplight Restaurant.

Above right: Side wall of the Lamplight Restaurant.

road with structures that were side-on. Characteristically, the courtyards were accessed through arched entrance ways. Given that timbers in the Lamplight Restaurant have been dated as 1493 and that the current geometry of the rest of Victoria Square is identical to that shown on the sixteenth-century map, it is more than likely that further investigations of the internal structure of buildings in this area would reveal yet more Tudor timbering.

After leaving Victoria Square, Tony and I moved on to Natural Choice in St John Street, a health food shop run by Steve Porter, who has been one of the driving forces behind the campaign to promote Ashbourne as a 'Fairtrade Town'. The interior of Steve's shop features a superb cruck beam of 1526, which was strengthened at a later date by the addition of a vertical support that allowed the front bay to be raised and the roof to be reorientated to run parallel with the street. This is one of two cruck beams that Tony has discovered to date in Ashbourne. The second one is located in the party wall between Ivan Spurrier-Smith's antique shop and the adjacent building in Church Street.

Natural Choice is flanked by Ashbourne's famous Gingerbread Shop, where the half-timbering visible on the façade looks genuinely old. However, this has not always been the case. Tony told me that the building had been 'modernised' in the eighteenth century, when the original timbers were covered over by render and the mullioned windows were replaced by sash windows. A century later, the Victorians gave the building a 'medieval' facelift by adding mock half-timbering to the render that had masked the genuine Tudor half-timbering in the first place!

Some years ago, at a time when Tony was still working as an architect, he was asked to draw up plans for the stripping away of these two layers of 'improvements' so that the original timbers could be revealed. When the restoration work was completed, the exposed timber-framing was dated by dendrochronology as 1492. The old Gingerbread shop now has the appearance of a genuine example of the type of 'gingerbread architecture' that is found in England's best-preserved Tudor towns.

DID YOU KNOW?

Dendrochronology, used to date the timbers in Ashbourne's old buildings, is based on the analysis of tree rings, also known as growth rings. Many trees make one growth ring per year. The thin inner portion of a ring is formed in the spring when growth is rapid and the thicker outer portion is formed in the summer. The number of rings provides a means of dating the timber; the thickness of each ring gives an indication of climatic conditions at the time.

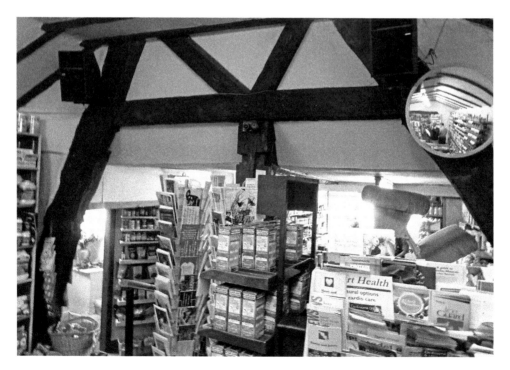

Interior of Natural Choice.

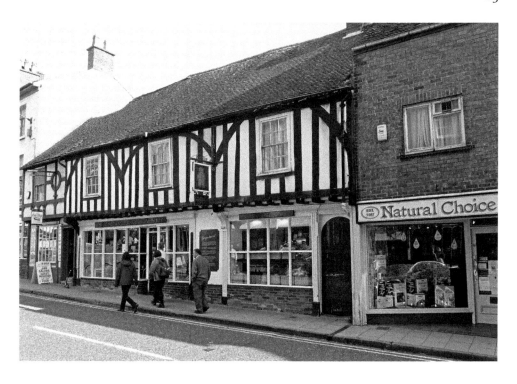

Above: The Gingerbread Shop.

Right: Mock timbering on the façade of the Cob Stop.

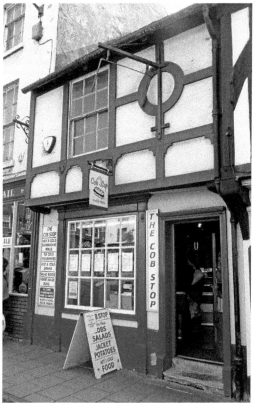

Unfortunately, render and fake-timbering still cover the original façade of the Cob Shop, a building that stands next door to the Gingerbread Shop, but old timber beams have been exposed in its interior. It is more than likely that explorations beneath the surface of the many other premises in the town would uncover yet more timber beams. Given the results of the limited investigations that have been carried out to date by Tony Short, it is already very clear that many of Ashbourne's buildings should not be taken at face value. Beneath the surface of the fine red-brick frontages that have given the town its reputation as a treasure house of Georgian architecture, there is ample evidence of equal architectural splendour from an earlier age.

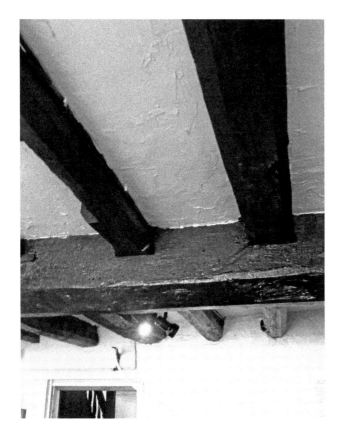

Genuine timbering in the interior of the Cob Stop.

3. Bakewell's Secret Ingredients

Derbyshire's most-famous culinary tradition is the Bakewell pudding. The origin of this unique dish can be traced back to the 1860s, when a group of noblemen who were dining at the White Horse Inn (now the Rutland Arms) asked if they could be served with a strawberry tart. Misunderstanding the instructions she had received, the cook spread an egg and almond mixture on top of strawberry jam, rather than stirring the mixture into the pastry. Instead of attracting complaints from the diners, the accidental dish was an instant hit.

The sequel to this episode is less clear-cut. According to the proprietors of the Old Original Bakewell Pudding Shop, which occupies premises formerly used by a candle maker, the recipe for the new dessert was acquired by the candle maker's wife, who began selling the pudding at her husband's shop, claiming that her recipe contained a special ingredient known only to her. Thanks to this clever ploy, customers were soon waxing more lyrically about her pudding than her husband's candles.

However, the proprietors of the nearby Bloomers Bakery claim that it is their product that is 'the only original Bakewell pudding', because it is based on a secret recipe that may have been handed down by a lady called Mrs Greaves to a gentleman called Mr Radford,

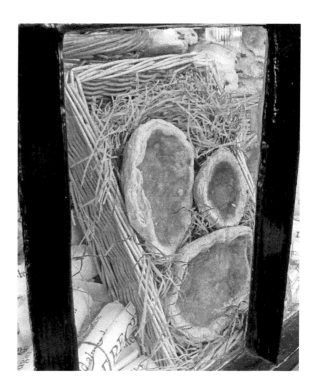

Bakewell pudding.

who may have passed it to Mr Bloomer, the founder of their shop. Yet another source of the famous pudding is the Bakewell Pudding Parlour, which has been making puddings according to its own recipe for over twenty years.

These rival claims not only add to the mystique surrounding the dish, but also help to draw visitors from far and wide to Bakewell, which has the additional advantage of occupying a beautiful location at the heart of the Peak District National Park. Given the familiarity of the town to so many visitors, it might be thought that there is nothing new to add to existing descriptions of the place. In fact, a careful exploration reveals that there are many secret ingredients that make Bakewell such a tasty visitor attraction.

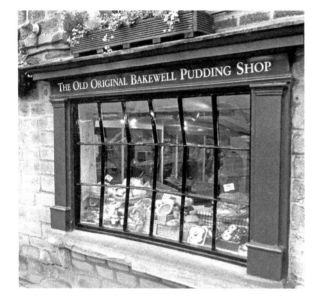

The Old Original Bakewell Pudding Shop.

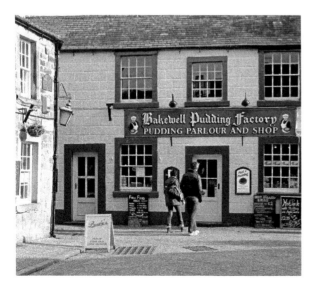

Bakewell Pudding Factory.

DID YOU KNOW?

Bakewell pudding should not be confused with Bakewell tart. The traditional pudding, comprising a puff pastry shell and a layer of jam covered with a filling of eggs, sugar, butter and almond, dates from a dish first produced by accident in the town more than 150 years ago. Bakewell tart is a much more recent invention, which has a shortcrust pastry shell, spread with jam and covered with a sponge-like filling, enriched with ground almonds.

The first surprise that strikes observant visitors is that the fabric of the town is very different from the limestone of the White Peak and the grey gritstone of the Dark Peak. Bakewell's texture is more akin to Cotswold stone, particularly when early morning sunlight gives the buildings a honey-coloured appearance. All Saints' Parish Church, which dominates the town from a prominent hill, looks particularly fine under this illumination, almost as if a miracle has enabled it to be bathed in a heavenly glow. Early plans for twin west towers on the church were never carried out, allowing the single, magnificent octagonal spire to be the crowning glory of the town.

The church is also known for its many memorials to the Vernon and Manners families, who were merged in romantic fashion when Dorothy Vernon fled from Haddon Hall to elope with John Manners, with the fugitives hurrying over the county border into Leicestershire where they were married in secret. It is said that Sir George Vernon, who had inherited Haddon Hall in 1515 and was known as the 'King of the Peak', had not been best pleased when Dorothy, his heiress, had declared her intention to marry John

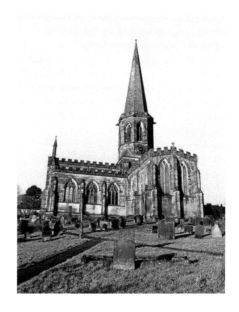

All Saints' Parish Church in early morning light.

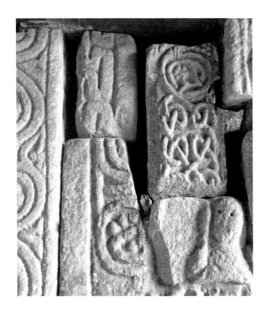

Saxon and Norman grave slabs.

Manners, who was not even a knight and was only the second son of the Earl of Rutland, who lived at Belvoir Castle in Leicestershire. However, on the death of Sir George in 1567, Haddon passed to John and Dorothy, with the hall becoming part of the Manners' estates, as it remains to this day.

Aside from the great octagonal spire and the memorials to the Vernon and Manners families, the church has a less well-known attraction. The south porch contains a remarkably extensive collection of elaborately carved Saxon and Norman grave slabs, crosses and figureheads. Many of these fragments were found in the foundations during the extensive restoration and rebuilding of the church in the 1840s. As David Hey points out in his book *Derbyshire: A History*, they form 'the largest and most varied collection of this kind in the country'.

Hey identifies some of the symbols on the twelfth- and thirteenth-century grave slabs as being 'a sword for a knight, shears for a wool merchant, a bugle horn for a Peak Forest warden, a bow and arrow for an archer and a chalice for a priest'. These slabs, crosses and figureheads are so tightly stacked that the porch has the appearance of a very well-stocked architectural antique shop.

A narrow passage beyond the churchyard leads to a sudden confrontation with a very imposing sixteenth-century yeoman's dwelling, which now houses the Old House Museum. Beamed rooms with great open fireplaces contain many fascinating reminders of past life in the town, including a fine historical toy collection, a Tudor toilet, and a Victorian privy!

A derelict building adjacent to the Old House Museum was once a row of cottages built by Sir Richard Arkwright for his workers at Lumford Mill. The ruined shell of the cottages now contains an open-air cut-out model of a former occupant engaged in the cleaning of raw cotton. Tucked away in the higher reaches of Bakewell, the museum and the former Arkwright site are secrets that remain undetected by many visitors, but they deserve to be on every tourist's itinerary.

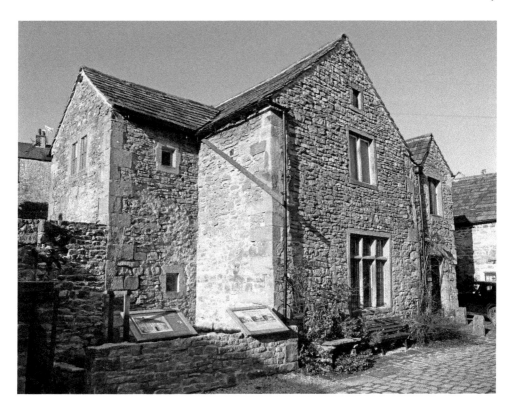

Old House Museum.

The original town of Bakewell was a hillside settlement, but the centre of gravity has now shifted down the hill to the level land by the river. The buildings in the lower town are largely eighteenth and nineteenth century, supplemented with some sympathetic modern additions, all fashioned in a pleasing country classical style. Bridge Street is lined with stone buildings that combine Georgian symmetry and classical detailing with older motifs such as mullions, transoms and lintels. The scale is modest but very pleasing on the eye.

But there is a very surprising ingredient in this architectural concoction. With its miniature gables and twin-light mullions, the seventeenth-century Market Hall looks much more like the buildings that surround the church than the other buildings in the lower town, as if it had been carried from the hill, glacier-like, when the town began to flow downhill. While the exterior of the building has been carefully preserved, the interior has been completely refashioned to house the excellent Peak Park Information Centre.

The Market Hall is a testimony to Bakewell's importance as a market town. The market charter was granted in 1330 and the tradition of a weekly Monday market continues to this day. When the stall market is in full flow in the town centre, a livestock market takes place across the river in a modern purpose-built hall. The building is yet another surprising architectural ingredient, because the hall is topped off by roof pods that look like Arabian tents, but are actually acoustic devices to reduce the noise emanating from the animals below.

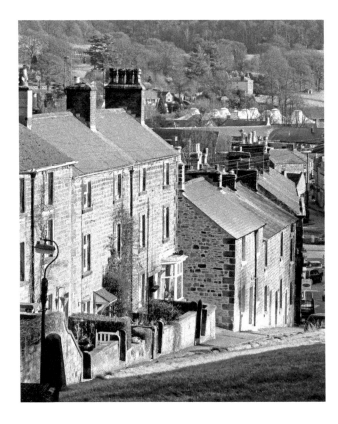

Looking towards the 'Arabian tents' of the livestock market.

Adjacent to the livestock market, there is an agricultural business centre and a café selling big breakfasts that are fit for farmers and for anyone else who enjoys a hearty meal. And on the last Saturday of every month, there is a farmers' market.

On every day of the week, and in every season, the town centre attracts a huge number of visitors. Many of those who come regularly may think that they know the place very well, but the area contains many secrets that are waiting to be discovered by observant visitors, because it is a warren of alleyways and courtyards with a wonderful range of independent and specialist shops.

One place that is certainly worth seeking out is Hebden Court, off Matlock Street, which has the delightful appearance of a Dickensian courtyard. Within this picturesque

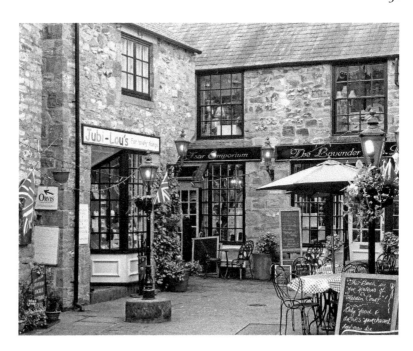

Hebden Court.

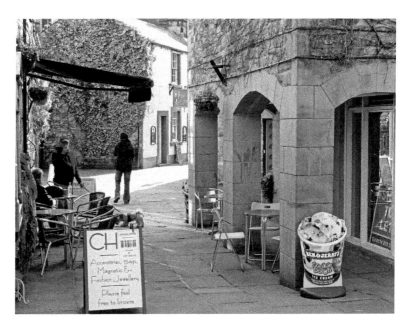

Portland Square.

little enclave, at the time of writing, there was a fabulous chocolate shop, a craft and interiors shop, various gift and clothes shops, a fly-fishing shop and a very inviting tea room. As Emily Roper and Shelly Pilkington of Beau, a little emporium selling ladies' fashion accessories, pointed out: 'Those visitors who never find their way to this little courtyard are missing out on a place that is very special'.

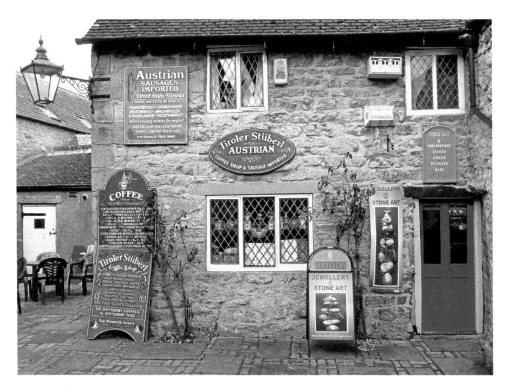

A touch of Austria.

All Bakewell's other courtyards, small squares and arcades merit exploration. For example, Granby Arcade, a winding alleyway of shops with façades of uniform appearance, has goods on sale ranging from cards, gifts and computer parts to stamps and jewellery. One shop offers the highly unusual combination of pet supplies and auto parts, and at the time of writing there was even a 'Bali Corner' in the arcade.

A hidden pedestrian alley running off Granby Road at the heart of the town is the unexpected location for Bakewell's swimming pool. Nearby Portland Square has a stone arcade that looks as if it has been lifted straight out of a painting by the Italian surrealist Giorgio de Chirico. Its shops include ladies' accessories and the Wee Dram, with its extensive collection of whiskies.

Two premises standing side by side on Water Street are a further illustration of the eclectic choice of goods available in the town, including products not normally associated with the Peak District. Tiroler Stüberl sells a huge range of imported Austrian foods, while the adjacent Stone Art Jewellery has items made from Whitby jet as well as from Derbyshire Blue John stone.

Bakewell has a great choice of coffee shops, tea rooms and pubs. An ice-cream van does a roaring trade with the many visitors who enjoy relaxing on the banks of the River Wye, even though their peace is likely to be disturbed when the river's abundant bird population spots the chance of being offered titbits and takes off en masse as though auditioning for a scene from Alfred Hitchcock's film *The Birds*.

DID YOU KNOW?

The Dukes of Rutland attempted to develop Bakewell into a spa to rival the spa of the Dukes of Devonshire at Buxton. As Bakewell is 183 metres lower in altitude than Buxton, they should have had a clear advantage, but the place never really grew into a fully fledged spa. The Bath House constructed in 1607 was fed by warm spa water, but its pool room is now the cellar of the British Legion Social Club.

In this age of Amazon, the town is fortunate in having several bookshops including Maxwell's on Granby Road and the well-known Bakewell Bookshop on Matlock Street, although the latter does now use half of its premises as a café. A second-hand bookshop, located at the entrance to the famous ancient bridge over the River Wye, has also managed to survive, but, as manager Margaret Wood explains, 'The shop was saved from closure because it was acquired by Bakewell and Eyam Community Transport, which uses the takings to support their community bus services. The shop is run by a team of fifteen volunteers who are motivated by their love of books and their wish to preserve this much-valued transport service, which has been under threat due to financial cutbacks.'

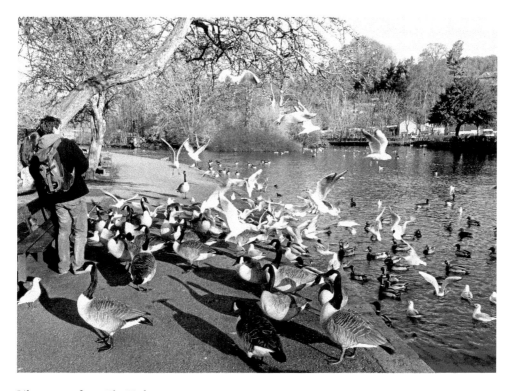

Like a scene from *The Birds*.

At the time of writing, another group of volunteers is busily drawing up plans to extend Peak Rail's heritage railway service from Rowsley to Bakewell, an ambitious scheme that would involve the construction of a new bridge over the A6, the laying of new tracks and extensive fencing and drainage work. If the extension goes ahead, it would bring yet more visitors to explore Bakewell, a town whose many secret ingredients make it such an appetising tourist and shopping destination.

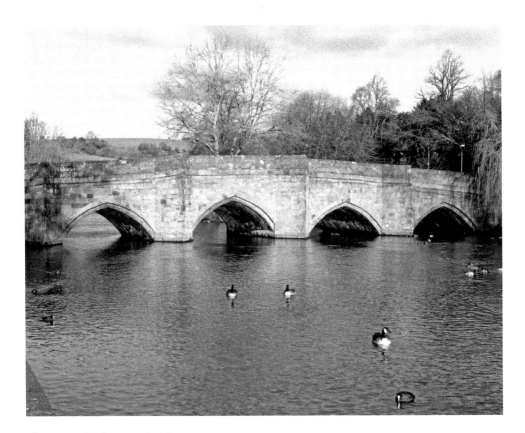

The ancient bridge over the Wye.

4. Secrets of Well Dressing and Exposing Tideswell's Hidden Gems

The origin of the ancient art of well dressing is uncertain. The practice of decorating wells with pictures made from flower petals and other natural materials is said to have begun in the village of Tissington in the fourteenth century, perhaps as a thanksgiving at the time of the Black Death for the purity of water sourced from local wells. Another theory contends that the practice started as an expression of gratitude for an uninterrupted supply of well water in a period of drought. In modern times, this long-standing Peak District custom attracts thousands of visitors to villages where the wells are 'dressed' in this way.

Some villages, but not all, are happy to reveal the secrets of well dressing to visitors by allowing them to witness the various stages involved in the preparation of their dressings. Traditionally, the process begins with a rather messy procedure called 'puddling'. This involves a 'puddler', suitably clad in a pair of stout wellington boots, tramping about in a soggy mixture of clay and water until the damp clay achieves the right consistency and uniformity.

Although it is now possible for 'dressers' to purchase ready-puddled clay from an enterprising firm in Stoke-on-Trent, some villages still use the traditional method. Whatever the means of preparation, the puddled clay is scooped into a wooden frame, where it is held in place by nails protruding from the base of the frame. It is then trowelled to create a perfectly smooth surface.

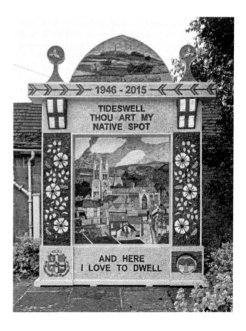

Tideswell well dressing.

Meanwhile, a local artist draws a picture on a very large piece of paper, which is then placed on the smooth surface of the damp clay. The outline of the composition is then 'pricked out' by using a needle, so that the image is transmitted from the paper to the surface of the clay in readiness for 'petalling'.

Petalling involves filling in the spaces between the outlines of the picture by pressing petals and other natural materials, such as leaves, bark and stone, onto the clay. This is a very meticulous operation, involving teams of 'dressers' working for several days until the picture is completely 'coloured in'. The frames are then hoisted into a vertical position, where they will stay throughout 'Well Dressing Week', so everyone can admire the colourful compositions that have been created so painstakingly.

Each village has its own traditional Well Dressing Week, held at some point in the period between May and September, and many places exhibit a number of dressings at different locations, thereby transforming their village into an outdoor art gallery. The visitors who flock to these exhibitions are invariably transfixed not only by the intricacy of the compositions, but also by the various materials used in their production, from the employment of dried rhubarb leaves for stonework to the use of hydrangea petals to 'paint' depictions of summer skies.

With regard to subject matter, some places concentrate on biblical themes, others use their dressings to commemorate significant anniversaries and many villages prefer to create pictures of local scenes. The main well dressing in the village of Tideswell, on display in the last week in June, almost invariably shows a majestic church surrounded by buildings that are characteristic of 'Olde England'.

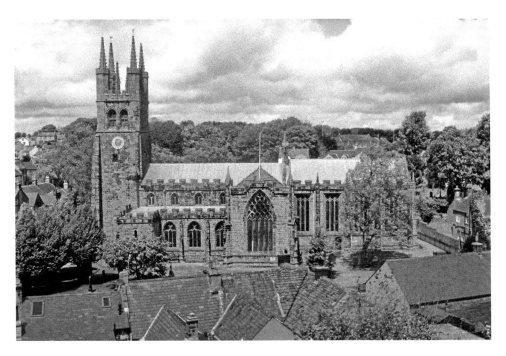

Tideswell Church – the 'Cathedral of the Peak'.

DID YOU KNOW?

For many years the custom of well dressing was confined to villages in the White Peak, but it has now been adopted by many villages in the Dark Peak. A number of places in the neighbouring counties of Staffordshire, South Yorkshire and Cheshire have also jumped onto the bandwagon. Dressings have now begun to appear in Much Wenlock in Shropshire and Malvern in Warwickshire, and Tom Shaw, a Derby man, even organised a well dressing in Perth in 1984 after emigrating to Australia.

The well-dressers of Tideswell often choose to illustrate a great cathedral in one of our ancient cities, but they return time and again for inspiration to the great church that stands in the centre of their very own village. The Church of St John the Baptist is not actually classed as a cathedral, but its magnificence has earned it the undisputed title of the 'Cathedral of the Peak'.

Tideswell's church is a wonderfully unified building, because it has not been subjected to any significant external changes since it was constructed all-of-a-piece in the fourteenth century, during those decades when the Decorated style was just beginning to evolve into the Perpendicular style. Surprisingly grand in scale for a church that serves a small former market town, the building has huge windows, a continuous line of battlements and a beautiful multi-pinnacled tower that perfectly counterbalances the enormous combined length of the nave and chancel.

Seen from within, the church is equally impressive, because the interior is very spacious and is flooded with light that streams in through the large, straight-headed windows of the chancel. As well as being celebrated for its grand proportions, the building is known for its extensive collection of highly unusual carvings fashioned by members of the local Hunstone family. Now, thanks to a project carried out by a local photographer called Bernard O'Sullivan, it has become clear that there is even more fascination in the interior of this magnificent building than meets the eye.

Bernard runs a multiple award-winning business that provides photographs for commercial, industrial and architectural clients. Although much of his work is based in the Manchester area, he and his wife, a senior lecturer at Manchester Metropolitan University, decided a few years ago to relocate from the city to Tideswell. The move was largely prompted by their wish to give Bernard's ninety-year-old father-in-law, who lived with the couple at that time, the experience of returning to his roots in the Peak District village.

Shortly after moving to the village, Bernard decided to put his photographic skills to use for the benefit of the village in a way that would also give him a chance to make himself known to the villagers. He came up with the idea of creating a large, highly detailed photograph that would illustrate the intricate beauty of the interior of the Cathedral of the Peak with so much clarity that features that had been largely hidden from view would be revealed for the first time.

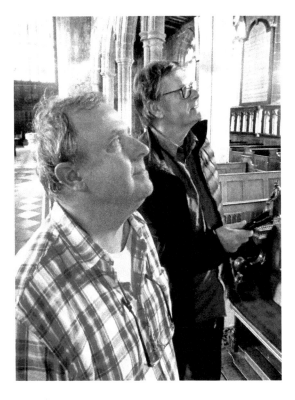

Left: Bernard O'Sullivan and Paul Black in Tideswell Church.

Below: Nave of Tideswell Church. (Photo: Bernard O'Sullivan)

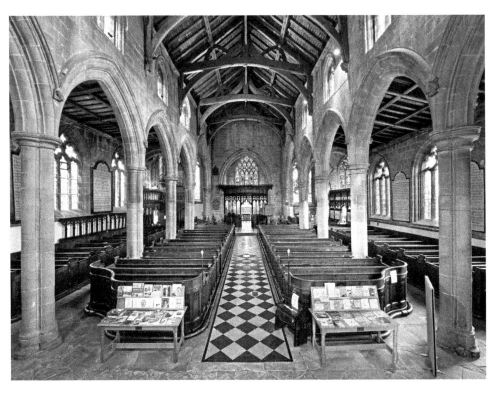

Using powerful flashlights and a camera suspended on a boom positioned halfway between the floor and the ceiling of the church, Bernard took multiple shots of the interior, all taken from the same position but in various states of illumination. By combining the images, he was able to make a single photograph of the nave that is clear in every detail.

When it became obvious to Bernard that his photograph had revealed carvings and other details that are not easily apparent to the naked eye, he decided that he would extend his project by taking a series of close-up photographs of each of these hidden gems. Slides of the pictures he took are now exhibited quite regularly in various venues in the Peak District. Usually, they are presented as part of a performance that includes contextual music and a commentary scripted by churchwarden Paul Black, a retired headteacher, who supplemented his research into the church's history by tapping the considerable expertise of local historians Alan Thornton and Dennis Ibbotson.

Bernard and Paul's presentation begins with interior shots taken from the base of the tower. These photographs expose a number of details in the roof that would be easily missed if the ceiling were to be viewed with the naked eye. One shot reveals very clearly that an inscription on the underside of a trapdoor in the ringing chamber includes the names of the churchwardens in 1812. Another close-up photograph highlights a mirror-written script on a shield in the stone vaulting. Why the letters should have been deliberately disguised in this clever way is not known.

The presentation moves on to Bernard's images of the nave's ceiling. These shots reveal a series of wooden carvings hidden among the roof timbers. One photograph shows a very

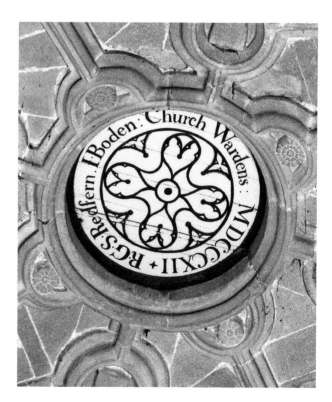

Carving on the
underside of a trapdoor.
(Photo: Bernard O'Sullivan)

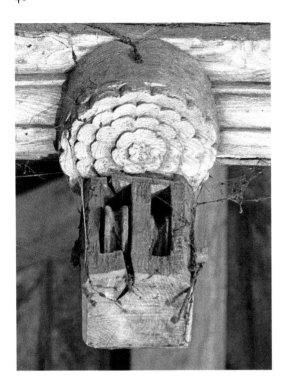

A roof pulley. (Photo: Bernard O'Sullivan)

odd Humpty Dumpty-like figure, while another picture reveals the presence of a wooden pulley. Paul thinks that this device could have been used to lift or lower a chandelier, whereas Bernard speculates that it could have been employed to suspend a metal vessel for holding incense.

The beauty of the nave is surpassed by the high and wide chancel, brightly illuminated by light from its large square-headed windows. Blinded by this overall effect, visitors often fail to spot the carvings of wooden angels on the ceiling. As Bernard's pictures show, these carvings are painted in bright colours and closely resemble the well-known images of angels found in chancels in East Anglia.

Whereas the paint used on the carved angels has faded over time, the stained-glass windows in the church have retained most of their colour. To capture the full glory of these windows, Bernard used a camera suspended on a boom in order to avoid the distortion of images that always arises whenever stained-glass windows are viewed from below.

Commenting on Bernard's pictures of a window that was designed as a memorial to the mothers of Revd Fletcher and his wife Mary, Paul said, 'Revd Fletcher was the vicar of Tideswell from 1900 to 1906. To my eyes, the style of this memorial window reflects the lingering influence of the Pre-Raphaelites, who had been so active in the previous century.'

Many of Bernard's photographs concentrate on the wonderful woodcarvings made by several generations of the Hunstone family. Bernard said, 'Although many of these carvings have details that are reasonably clear to the naked eye, some are more difficult to decipher because they are permanently in shade. I wanted to illustrate all the Hunstone carvings in the best possible light because they contain such a profusion of images.'

DID YOU KNOW?

When the celebrated artist John Piper boasted that he had worked in every medium available to him, a Sheffield man called Malcolm Nix asked him if he had ever designed a well dressing. When Piper admitted that he had not done so, he took on the task of designing a well picture for Youlgrave in 1979. His drawing of a scary-looking man, possibly intended to represent a green man, proved to be difficult to dress, indicating that well pictures are probably best left to locals who are familiar with the traditional techniques of dressing.

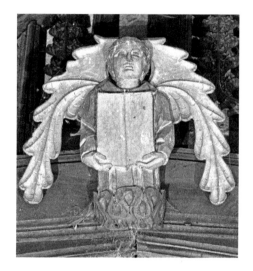

An angel carving in the roof.
(Photo: Bernard O'Sullivan)

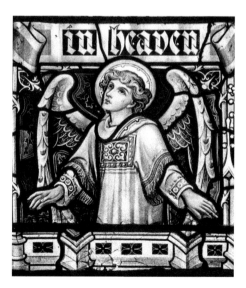

Detail of the west window.
(Photo: Bernard O'Sullivan)

The earliest carvings were created in 1895 by Advent Hunstone, a local stonemason who had been asked by Canon Andrew if he might be able to turn his hand from stonemasonry to woodcarving, which would enable him to decorate a casing for a new organ that had been installed in the church. He was also asked to create a carved screen that would divide the organ from the Lady chapel. Advent, who ran his business in partnership with his brother Robert, took up this new challenge with enthusiasm and, in no time at all, the brothers began to show remarkable skill and creativity in producing woodcarvings of outstanding originality and individuality.

The Hunstone carvings are described in an excellent booklet, which is on sale in the church. This informative publication was written by Canon Martin Hulbert, who pointed out that the organ casing and the screen are decorated with no fewer than twenty-two wooden arches. Each arch contains seven or nine carved motifs, making over 150 motifs in all, quite apart from the many carved heads above the arches. Marvelling at this profusion of images, Canon Hulbert asks: 'Where did the craftsmen begin with such an enormous task? What richness lies ahead for those with time to study the work in detail? Many of the motifs are leaves and flowers, birds and animals. It almost becomes a study in botany and zoology, and very few motifs are repeated.'

The canon's point is well illustrated by the staggering variety of the carvings on two of the arches on the chancel screen. One arch features carved images of a dragon, an elephant, a boar, a hippopotamus, a bear, a rhinoceros and a pelican feeding its chicks; the other arch contains depictions of a clover leaf, a holly leaf, a blackberry leaf, a primrose,

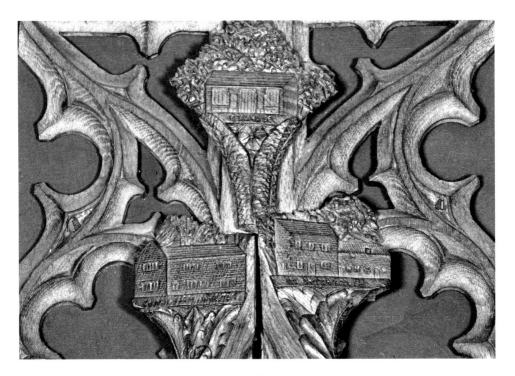

Detail of the organ carvings. (Photo: Bernard O'Sullivan)

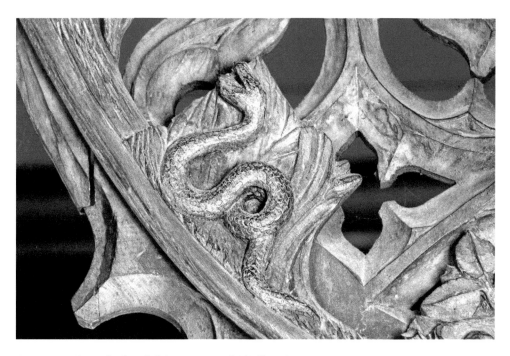

Carvings in the Lady chapel. (Photo: Bernard O'Sullivan)

a lily of the valley, a dock leaf and a five-petal flower. Mixed in with the multiple images of flora and fauna on the organ case and screen, there are depictions of angels, saints and various bishops, along with images of local churches and schools and representations of Lichfield Cathedral and Southwell Minster.

There is a further set of remarkable Hunstone carvings on the end of the choir stalls including some particularly tender and moving images. They represent holy baptism, confirmation, ordination, the visitation of the sick, the care of the young, growing up in the church, prayer and praise. Although additional carvings in the chancel were carved by Tooly of Bury St Edmunds, the lectern, with its fine eagle's head, was produced by the Hunstones, as was the intricately carved vicar's chair under the pulpit.

Advent Hunstone's switch from stonemasonry to woodcarving marked the beginning of a tradition of woodcarving in Tideswell that was kept alive by four generations of the Hunstone family. When the fame of the carvings spread, Advent began receiving so many commissions from other churches that he had to recruit a number of local people to his workforce, including his two nephews, William and 'Young Advent'.

In 1923, when Old Advent's health began to deteriorate, Young Advent took over the firm and remained in charge until his retirement in 1960. His place at the helm was then taken by William's son, Bill, who had first joined the family firm in the 1950s. Bill's son, Michael, also became involved with the firm, which continued to produce ecclesiastical furnishings until Bill's death in 1987.

Even without the benefit of special photography, the amazing legacy left by the Hunstone family will be revealed to any observant visitor to the Cathedral of the Peak

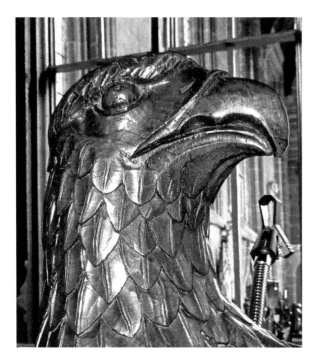

An eagle's head lectern.

but, thanks to the brilliant fine detail of Bernard O'Sullivan's photographs, the full glory of the Hunstone carvings, including those that are difficult to decipher with the naked eye, has now been exposed.

DID YOU KNOW?

The impressive dimensions of the 'Cathedral of the Peak' in Tideswell are an indicator of the village's former importance as a medieval market centre for trade in wool, livestock and lead. Tideswell was first granted a market charter in 1251. Neville Sharpe, a local historian, believes that the steps that support the sundial in the churchyard may have been the base of the original market cross.

Bernard's photographs also draw attention to several other carvings in the church that are often overlooked. These include various depictions of the green man and a carving of a small heraldic winged lion. And there are several examples of graffiti featuring the letters 'A.M'. These are said to represent Ave Maria and were probably carved to invoke the protection of the Virgin Mary.

Two memorials highlighted by Bernard's photographs are of particular interest. One is located on a pillar in the south aisle and is dedicated to George Oldfield. It is fashioned in a rare type of black marble found near the Peak District village of Ashford-in-the-Water. It was carved by White Watson, the distinguished geologist and author of the classic book *Strata of Derbyshire*. Another memorial is dedicated to Bishop Pursglove, the founder of Tideswell Grammar School. Explaining why the bishop is depicted in pre-Reformation vestments, Paul Black said, 'The bishop was described in his lifetime as being "stiff in papistry" and was deprived of his position as Suffragan Bishop of Hull because he refused to acknowledge the monarch as head of the church.'

As Bernard's photographs show, a close inspection of the Cathedral of the Peak will uncover a wealth of fascinating detail. On your next visit to the great church, train your eyes on the ceiling until you are able to focus on the extraordinary inscriptions lurking in the vaults, wooden carvings hidden among the roof timbers and visions of angels flying above the chancel. Search every nook and cranny of the screen of the Lady chapel and the casing of the organ until you become lost in a wondrous world of flora and fauna; allow yourself to be moved by the tender carvings at the end of the choir stalls and be dazzled by the kaleidoscopic colour of the stained-glass windows.

Reflect on the discoveries you have made in the Cathedral of the Peak, or prepare for your next visit by attending an exhibition of Bernard O'Sullivan's photographs, accompanied by Paul Black's commentary. Their joint presentation is likely to feature as one of the events scheduled for the most important week in Tideswell's calendar, which is, of course, its annual Wakes and Well Dressing Week.

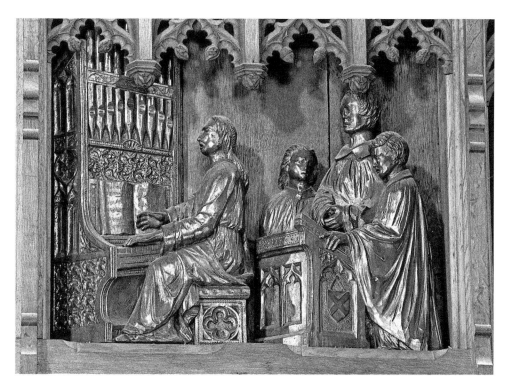

Hunstone carving of the organist and the choir.

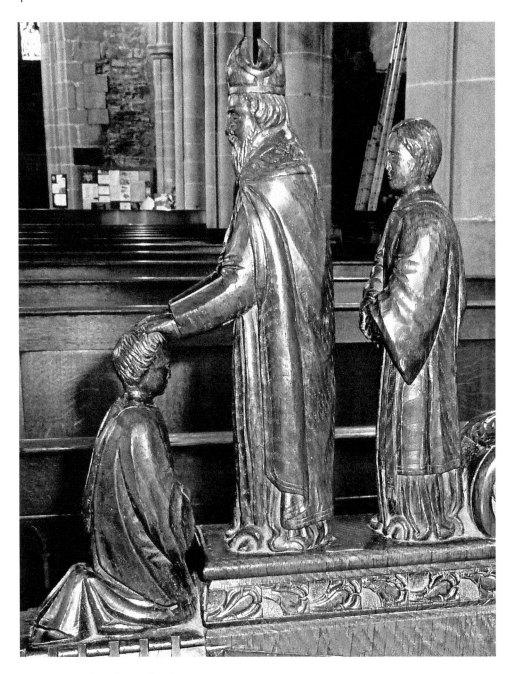

Hunstone carving of an ordination.

Part Two

The Secrets of the Hills and Dales

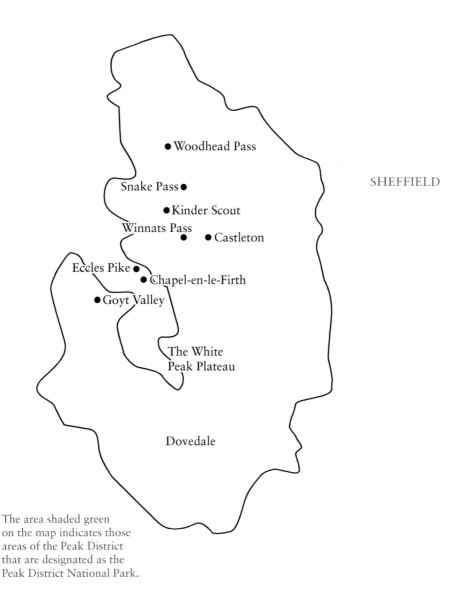

Woodhead Pass

SHEFFIELD

Snake Pass

Kinder Scout

Winnats Pass

Castleton

Eccles Pike

Chapel-en-le-Firth

Goyt Valley

The White
Peak Plateau

Dovedale

The area shaded green
on the map indicates those
areas of the Peak District
that are designated as the
Peak District National Park.

5. Grand Illusions

Anyone scanning a contour map of the British Isles for areas of spectacular upland scenery would be unlikely to pick out the Peak District. Upland Britain is already giving way to lowland England in this most southerly region of the Pennines. The hills of Peakland never rise above 650 metres, whereas at least a dozen summits in the Yorkshire Dales, just a few miles further up the Pennine Chain, exceed this height. And, if truth be known, there are actually very few hills in the Peak District that are worthy of being called 'peaks'. And yet...

More visitors are drawn to the Peak District National Park than to any other national park in the world, other than Mount Kyoto in Japan, and writers have been known to wax lyrically about the 'mountain' scenery of the area. Describing her vision of the Derbyshire Moors in *Jane Eyre*, Charlotte Brontë wrote, 'A north Midland shire, dusk with moorland, ridged with mountain, this I see.' And Lord Byron was even moved to claim, in a letter to the poet Thomas Moore, that there are 'things in Derbyshire as noble as in Greece or Switzerland'. Are these glowing descriptions merely poetic licence, or do they bear some relationship to reality?

The Peak may not amount to very much on a contour map, but the spectacular nature of the scenery is as obvious to today's visitors as it was to Charlotte Brontë and Lord Byron. Despite the relatively modest true dimensions, there is very clearly an illusion of grand scale. But what is the secret behind this deceit?

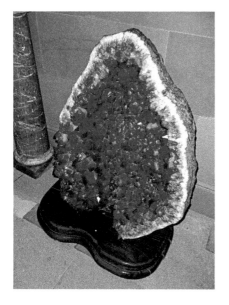

Blue John.

There is no better place in which to examine the relationship between true scale and apparent scale than the area around the tourist hotspot of Castleton. The village is known for its four great show caves. Blue John Cavern and Treak Cliff Cavern are the only sources in the world of Blue John, a dazzlingly coloured form of fluorspar much used for ornaments and jewellery. Fine examples of Blue John are to be seen in Castleton's many gift shops and in the wonderfully comprehensive Peak District National Park Information Centre in the village.

Speedwell Cavern is a former lead mine where visitors are taken by boat along an underground canal that leads to an enormous hole known as the 'Bottomless Pit'. Peak Cavern is entered through an awesome 20-metre-high gaping hole in an almost vertical cliff. Since the sixteenth century, the cavern had been known as the Devil's Arse until it was rechristened 'Peak Cavern' to spare the blushes of Queen Victoria when she attended a concert in one of the cave's vast chambers in 1880. Judging that people are not so easily embarrassed in this day and age, the present owners of the cave have now seen fit to revive the original name.

DID YOU KNOW?

Castleton's annual 'Garlanding Ceremony', which commemorates the restoration to the throne of Charles II in 1660, takes place on Oak Apple Day, 29 May. A local man is dressed as Charles II and a huge conical garland of flowers is placed over his head. Accompanied by his consort, a troupe of dancers and a band, he is paraded around the village on horseback, with the procession pausing at each of the six pubs in the village for refreshment. After his 'pub crawl', the king is relieved of his garland, which is then hoisted to the pinnacle of the church tower.

The geometry of these hugely popular subterranean attractions is remarkable enough, but the natural features found above ground in the Castleton area are no less spectacular. They provide some of the best examples in the Peak District landscape of the remarkable contrast between real scale and apparent scale.

The village of Castleton sits at the head of the Hope Valley, a beautiful dale that is closed off at its western extremity by Mam Tor, a hill popularly known as the 'Shivering Mountain'. At a mere 517 metres, Mam Tor hardly qualifies as a mountain, but its overall shape and its precipitous face, which is subject to frequent landslips, give it the appearance of a true mountain. After leaving Castleton, motorists head towards Mam Tor by taking a narrow road through the spectacular Winnats Pass, where the carriageway climbs a 1 in 5 gradient between towering crags.

However, the apparent physical grandeur of this miniature land of mountains and ravines is very fragile and has to be handled with great care, because illusions can be shattered so easily. The eye can only be deceived by hills with the conical shape of

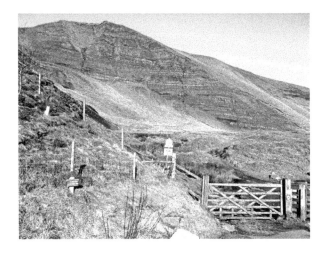

Mam Tor – the Shivering Mountain.

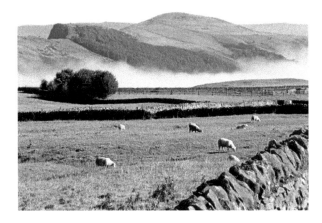

Back Tor and Lose Hill.

mountains and by ravines with the geometry of mountain passes if man-made objects in the landscape are deferentially small in scale. Large constructions, such as wide roads, high chimneys and electricity pylons, act as reference measures and provide a key to the real scale of the landscape.

In the presence of such intrusions, natural features lose their ability to deceive the eye. Winnats Pass is one of the most spectacular gorges in England, but it is an even more impressive sight today than it was in former years, not as a result of some change in the natural contours, but because an intrusive line of telegraph poles that once flanked the road through the pass has been removed. As old photographs show, the presence of these tall structures had the effect of reducing the vertical scale of the gorge.

Some years ago the pass came under renewed threat when it became clear that the turnpike road running up the side of Mam Tor had collapsed so badly that it was beyond repair. Serious consideration was given to a scheme to widen the road through Winnats Pass, in order to create a new major route out of the Hope Valley. Fortunately, the plan

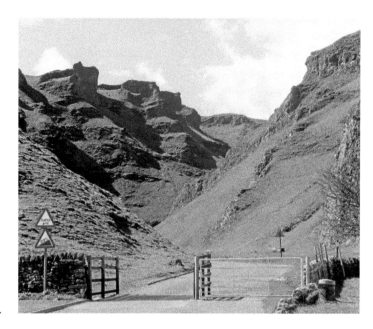

Entrance to Winnats Pass.

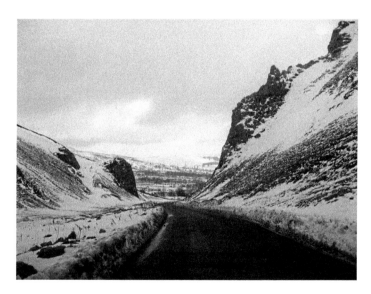

Winnats Pass in winter.

was rejected and the narrow, winding road remains, giving due emphasis to the height of the flanking crags and pinnacles.

From the summit of Mam Tor there is a superb view of Castleton and the Hope Valley. The planned Norman town of Castleton can be seen sitting neatly at the foot of a lofty crag surmounted by the keep of Peveril Castle, a formidable fortification built by Henry II in 1176. But it is the cement works, a couple of miles beyond Castleton, that catches the eye. The chimney of the works is so enormous that the surrounding hills have an apparent scale that is less than their real height.

DID YOU KNOW?

The Snake Pass links the Manchester conurbation with the towns and cities of South Yorkshire. Rising to 510 metres at its highest point, the pass is almost always the first road in England to be closed in winter due to snow. Although many people assume that the name of the pass is a reference to the countless twists and turns in the road, it actually refers to the serpent on the coat of arms of the 6th Duke of Devonshire who, together with the Duke of Norfolk, financed the building of the road in 1818.

Although the works were constructed in the days before the area received the protection of national park status, fierce lobbying by the Council for the Preservation of Rural England (now called the Campaign to Protect Rural England) forced the Ministry of Works to employ a landscape consultant to find ways of minimising the impact of the works.

The wide Hope Valley, with its ring of hills, is a superb composition. To have permitted unrestricted limestone extraction and processing would have been akin to vandalising an artist's masterpiece. Rampant quarrying would have created a giant's knife-cut in the landscape equivalent to a slash in a painting. To have allowed shale tailings to spill across the valley floor would have been like throwing paint at a canvas.

Sir Geoffrey Jellicoe, who was hired as the landscape consultant, drew up a fifty-year plan. He suggested that lakes and recreation areas could be made from shale excavations and he proposed that any new limestone quarries should emanate from just one narrow entrance in the hillside. These parts of Jellicoe's recommendations have been followed with some success.

Jellicoe was also concerned about the possible proliferation of buildings at the works. He suggested that all future constructions should be grouped within the existing complex.

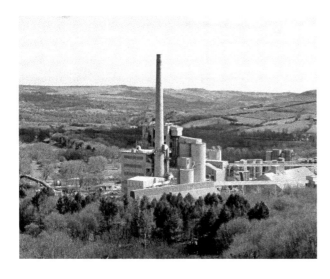

Hope Valley cement works.

Although development has indeed been confined to a restricted area, there have been some unfortunate consequences. All the buildings associated with the works now look as if they have been piled together and locked in a massive concrete cage. And the consultant did not envisage that the pair of 30-metre-high chimneys of the original works would be replaced by a single 120 metre-high chimney. As a result, the modern cement works stand in the Hope Valley like Gulliver in Lilliput!

Fortunately, there are some places in the valley where the cement works are largely hidden from view. From these favoured locations, the castle on its crag can make its presence felt, because the tall chimney of the works is no longer able to act as a measure of vertical scale. However, the commanding position of the castle is best appreciated from Cave Dale, a 'secret' valley immediately south of Castleton, where there are no intrusions to reduce the scale.

DID YOU KNOW?

572 kilometres of overhead power lines run through England's National Parks and Areas of Outstanding Natural Beauty. In 2014 the National Grid announced plans to remove ugly pylons from all our National Parks by resiting the power lines underground. Unfortunately, the 12 kilometres of disfiguring pylons that march across the Longdendale Valley in the northern Peak District were not identified in the first tranche of this scheme.

Tourists can visit Peveril Castle by undertaking an exhilarating walk up a steep zigzag path from Castleton. Looking out from the perimeter wall of the castle grounds, visitors are left in no doubt about the impregnability of the Norman fortification. Sheer cliffs fall away on all sides and there is a classic feudal relationship between castle and village. Although the buildings of Castleton form a picturesque group, they show due deference to the dominating position of the castle by being modest in scale. Even the tower of the ancient parish church of St Edmund's is suitably squat.

Land to the north of Castleton is dominated by the high moors and ridges of the Dark Peak. The vastness of the moors, which form the largest area of wilderness in England, is made all the more apparent by the absence of prominent man-made features on the moorland. However, two cross-Pennine routes traverse the region: the Snake Pass, which runs between the Kinder Scout plateau and Bleaklow Hill, and the more northerly Woodhead Pass, which separates Bleaklow from the moors of Saddleworth.

Motorway planners have long eyed the Woodhead Pass as a possible pathway for a Manchester–Sheffield motorway. If a six-lane highway were to be constructed across this region, the horizontal scale of the moors would be greatly reduced and the wilderness quality would be lost.

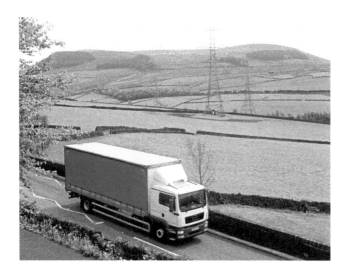

Woodhead Pass, with pylons marching across the Longdendale Valley.

The wilderness of these moors was so valued by ramblers seeking weekend escapes from the smoke-filled mill towns of Lancashire that they fought for access to this vast tract of high land by organising the famous 'Mass Trespass' on Kinder Scout in 1932. Their direct action campaign, in defiance of the landowners who refused entry to land they had reserved for grouse shooting, led eventually to the setting up, in 1951, of Britain's first national park in the Peak District, which includes Kinder Scout.

Another victory for access was the opening, in 1965, of the Pennine Way, Britain's first long-distance footpath, which runs from the Peak District to the Scottish Border, and is enjoyed, at least for part of its length, by no fewer than a quarter of a million walkers per year. The path starts at the village of Edale and continues its journey north through the Dark Peak by crossing over the Snake Pass and the Woodhead Pass.

As the Mass Trespassers knew all too well, there is no better place to escape from the stresses of everyday life than the high moors of the Dark Peak. The caravan and camping site at Crowden is a favourite base for exploring this great area of wilderness. In the words of the site warden, this is a place 'where people can live alongside nature'.

Unfortunately, the grand scale of the surrounding moorland in this particular part of the Woodhead Pass is reduced somewhat by the presence of a procession of gargantuan electricity pylons that march for 12 kilometres across the landscape, much like soldiers in an invading Brobdingnagian army. Thankfully, the National Grid intends to remove these intrusive overhead lines in the long term by rerouting them underground.

In marked contrast to the barren moors of the Dark Peak, the limestone plateau of the White Peak, to the south of Castleton, is a tamed and settled land; no moorland remains, and sheep and Friesian cattle graze in the enclosed fields. The colours of the plateau – the pastel green of the fields and the pale grey of the enclosure walls – are soft and easy on the eye.

The landscape is also softened by the copses of trees that cover many hillocks. Some of these trees are a legacy of man's early exploitation of the vast mineral wealth of the Peak District, because the farmers who doubled as lead miners were wise enough to surround their mine workings with clumps of trees to prevent their cattle from grazing on lead-polluted land.

DID YOU KNOW?

One of the most popular paintings in Sheffield's Graves Art Gallery is *Derbyshire Walls* by Harry Epworth Allen. Despite losing a leg in the First World War, the Sheffield artist made frequent trips into the Peak District to paint what he called 'the rhythmical bulges and depressions of the landscape'. This particular painting captures to perfection how the lattice of stone enclosure walls picks out and exaggerates the natural contours, converting bumps into hills and shallow depressions into valleys.

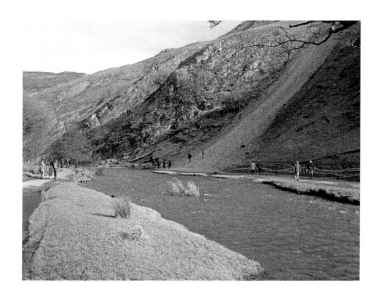

Dovedale in winter.

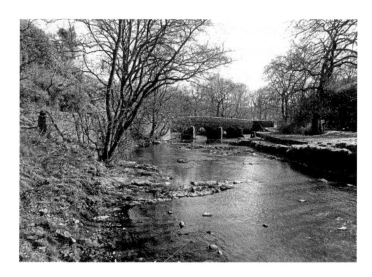

Manifold Valley.

The White Peak is also a source of high-quality limestone. The quarrymen of old helped to enhance the appearance of the area by making its stone available for refashioning into farm buildings, walls and villages, all of which fit into the landscape as easily as a rock outcrop. Of course, scars were left by this cosmetic operation, but these have largely healed because the early quarries were worked on a small scale. However, limestone is now extracted from huge quarries that leave vast open sores on the White Peak plateau. And the stone is no longer used primarily for local building. Today's quarrymen pillage the Peak: they blast its rock, crush it into aggregate and carry it away in hundreds of lorries for use in chemical plants and in the making of roads. Thankfully, these massive quarries are largely confined to areas outside the boundary of the Peak District National Park.

Fast-flowing rivers – the Dove, the Manifold and the Lathkill – have made deep indentations into the limestone plateau. These lush gorges have become honeypots for the

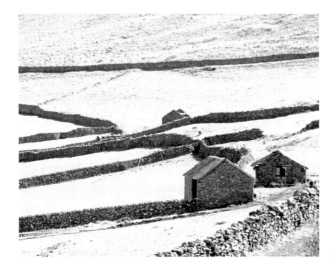

Near Castleton.

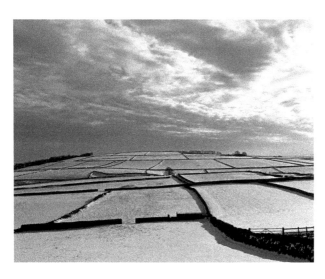

Stone walls in winter.

tourists who swarm to the area. Many visitors to Dovedale, rightly regarded as one of the most beautiful valleys in England, are content to walk along the banks of the fast-flowing Dove only as far as its famous stepping stones, but those who venture further up the steep-sided valley are rewarded by surprise encounters with caves and limestone pinnacles.

The plateau above these beautiful valleys attracts fewer visitors. It would seem that some of today's tourists share John Ruskin's view of the White Peak: 'The whole gift of the country is in its glens. The wide acreage of field and moor above is wholly without interest.' The Ward Lock guide to the Peak District is equally dismissive of the plateau, describing it as 'bleak and marred by many stone walls'.

When viewed from the air, it is true that the vast network of enclosure walls, with as many as 24 miles of wall for every square mile of farmland, imposes on the landscape a strict and repetitive geometry of rectangular field patterns. However, the picture is very different at ground level, where the eye is not aware of the regular patterns. Just as a covering net accentuates the writhing of a trapped animal, the stone walls pick out and exaggerate every change in contour on the plateau. Bumps are made into hills and potentially monotonous plains are shown to have interesting undulations and shallow valleys. Moreover, the stone walls cannot be seen as an intrusion on the landscape because they are made of the very stuff on which they stand. As all true lovers of the White Peak know, Ruskin's judgement was wrong: the wide acreage of field and moor above is wholly *with* interest.

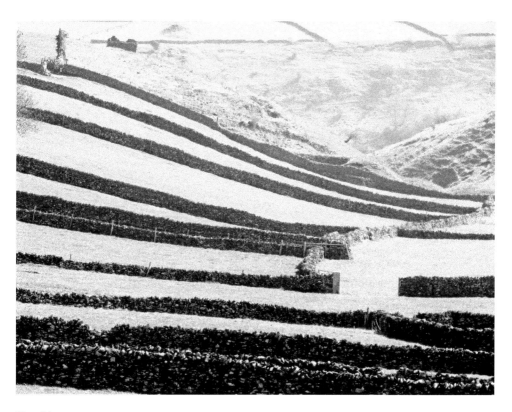

Near Litton.

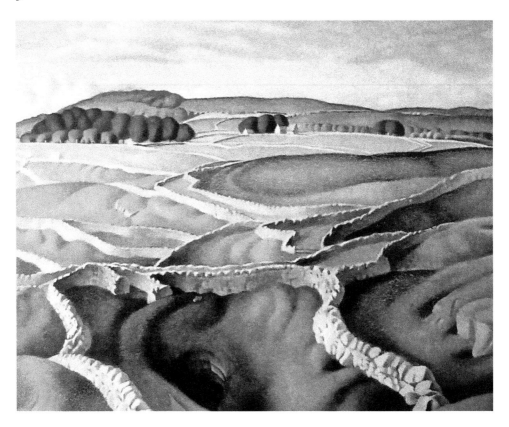

Derbyshire Walls by Harry Epworth Allen. (© Harry Epworth Allen Estate)

However, the dismissive words of Ruskin would be justified if the dismantling of some of the enclosure walls that has happened in recent years were allowed to continue, because any further removal would threaten to reduce the limestone plateau to a featureless, monotonous dome. These man-made additions to the natural landscape deserve greater protection, because they are the secret of the White Peak's considerable visual appeal.

In marked contrast, as we have seen, it is man-made additions that pose a threat to the Dark Peak. Wide roads, high chimneys, lofty pylons and large buildings reduce the apparent grandeur of the natural landscape that is the secret to the visual appeal of that part of the region. The message to planners and developers is clear: the White Peak and the Dark Peak are both beautiful Lilliputian lands, so please tread carefully to avoid damage.

6. The Secret History of the Goyt Valley

The sinuous road that crosses 6.5 kilometres of moorland between Buxton and Whaley Bridge is signposted as the A5004, but is more commonly known as 'Long Hill'. After leaving Buxton, the road climbs to a 427-metre summit of the aptly named Wild Moor, before descending in a series of twists and turns to Whaley Bridge. Favoured by motorcyclists recklessly seeking to challenge their driving skills, Long Hill has been named by the Road Safety Foundation as the seventh most dangerous road in Britain.

Although drivers using the A5004 need to keep their eyes firmly trained on the road ahead, they cannot avoid being aware of the extensive views to their left across the Goyt Valley, a long, deep ravine running parallel with Long Hill, but far below it.

Access to the valley can be obtained by leaving Long Hill at its summit and taking a left turn onto Goyt Lane, which runs for a short way across moorland before descending into the valley of the river Goyt in very dramatic fashion. Alongside this initial high-level stretch of the lane, there is a stone-built roadside shrine dedicated to the Blessed Virgin Mary. The isolated moorland setting of the shrine is captured to perfection in a painting in the collection of Buxton Museum and Art Gallery. This evocative landscape picture was created in the mid-twentieth century by an accomplished artist called Harry Kingsley, who was adept at capturing the wildness and remoteness of the moors.

The shrine was built in the 1950s at the instigation of Canon Baldwin of St Anne's Roman Catholic Church in Buxton. It stands between two old gateposts and is inset with a mosaic flanked by flowers, which are replenished on a regular basis. An inscription reads, 'Hail Mary full of grace; Mother of Jesus; Queen of the World; pray for us.' This

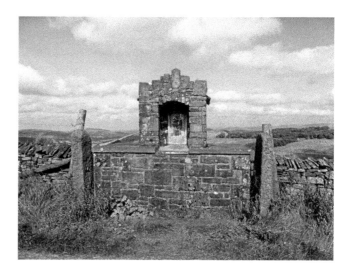

The shrine above the Goyt Valley.

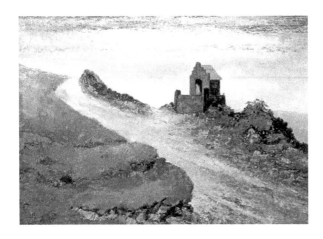

The Shrine by Harry Kingsley.
(Buxton Museum and Art Gallery)

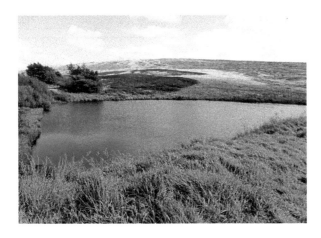

Reservoir above the incline.

shrine is the first clue to the romantic story of the Grimshawe family, which is recounted in fascinating detail in various books by Gerald Hancock.

The Grimshawes lived at Errwood Hall, their grand country mansion hidden in the depths of the Goyt Valley. Their pretentious hall was constructed in the 1830s by Samuel Grimshawe, a wealthy Manchester businessman. It was his son, the second Samuel Grimshawe, who contributed much of the money needed for the construction of St Anne's Church in 1860.

The first clue to the industrial past of the valley is provided by a small reservoir that is located alongside Goyt Lane immediately before the road drops down a 1-in-7 incline. The reservoir provided water for the steam engines and pulleys that hauled trains up and down the incline, which was constructed in the 1830s as part of the Cromford & High Peak Railway, designed to carry minerals and other goods from the canal wharf at Cromford on the western side of the Peak District hills to the canal basin at Whaley Bridge on the eastern side. As one of the highest railways in the country, this was one of the greatest of the many spectacular feats of Victorian engineering.

The steep incline was tarmacked over in 1967 and is now an arrow-straight road that descends from the moor towards Fernilee Reservoir, which appears as a shimmering sheet of water deep in the valley below. Completed in 1938 with a capacity of 4,940 million litres, the reservoir was built to supply drinking water to the town of Stockport and the surrounding districts. Nine farmsteads had to be demolished when this part of the Goyt Valley was flooded and the remains of several old industries were also washed away in the process, including the last vestiges of the Chilworth Gunpowder Works.

At the gunpowder works, charcoal, sulphur and saltpetre were ground up, pressed and broken into fragments to make explosives for use in the local quarries and coal mines. Almost 100 workers were employed in the factory, doing work that was fraught with danger. Between 1881 and 1893 there were over a dozen explosions, but the worst incident occurred in 1909 when three men were killed in a massive blast. Of course, most of the visitors who come today to enjoy walks around the reservoir are unaware of the tragic history that lies hidden beneath its tranquil waters.

In 1967 the Stockport Water Corporation completed a second reservoir in an adjacent, but slightly higher stretch of the Goyt Valley. The construction of Errwood Reservoir, with a capacity of 4,215 million litres, involved the flooding of the picturesque hamlet of Goyt's Bridge, once a favourite picnic spot for people living in the High Peak. My wife, who was born in nearby Chapel-en-le-Frith, can remember occasions in her childhood when she was woken early to travel with her family to this enchanted place to listen to the dawn chorus.

When the reservoir was built, the hamlet's iconic packhorse bridge was removed stone by stone and reconstructed over the River Goyt at a point in the valley above and beyond the reservoirs, allowing it to be the centrepiece once again of a popular beauty spot, albeit one in a different location in the dale of the Goyt.

DID YOU KNOW?

The River Goyt rises on Axe Edge, the last great hill of the Pennine Chain, before flowing down from the hills to join the River Tame at Stockport, so forming the River Mersey. In fact, the source of the Goyt on the Peak District moors could be considered to be the ultimate source of the Mersey.

The hamlet of Goyt's Bridge and several farmsteads in the area had been in the ownership of the Grimshawes of Errwood Hall. The family's grand house had ground-floor Venetian windows in two bays, a large Italianate central tower, and an entrance way topped by the family crest, featuring a dragon. The gardens had an ornamental archway and a fountain. When Mary Gosselin-Grimshawe, the last of the Grimshawes, died in 1930, most of the contents of the hall, accumulated by the family over the previous century, were sold at auction. The building itself survived for a short time and was used as a youth hostel, but its eventual demolition was prompted by fears that the two Goyt Valley reservoirs would be polluted if people were allowed to occupy any of the buildings in the immediate vicinity of the lakes.

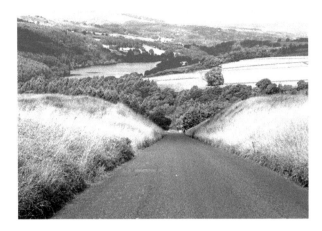

The incline.

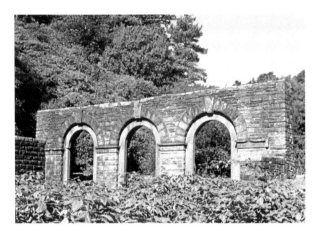

The ruins of Errwood Hall.

The site of the hall is reached by taking a steep path from the car park on the shores of Errwood Reservoir and then walking through woodland along a long former driveway until a plateau-like clearing is reached. This is the romantic location where the gaunt reminders of the once magnificent country residence are to be found. These comprise a scattering of foundation stones and the erect frames of four large ground-floor windows and one grand Venetian window. The carving of the family crest now lies forlornly on the ground beneath the ruins of entrance way that it once topped.

DID YOU KNOW?

For an area without any large natural lakes, it is surprising to find that three of the Peak Disrict's most visited areas are places containing artificial lakes: the Upper Derwent Dams, Carsington Reservoir and the Goyt Valley.

The remains may be sparse, but they are sufficient for the imagination to piece together the grand proportions of the house that once stood in this clearing in the woods. The voices of children who often play among the ruins sound like echoes of the wonderful parties that were held in the hall by the Grimshawes, not only for members of the gentry and other distinguished guests but also for the families of their estate workers and for people living in the surrounding settlements. The stories of guests coming up the snow-covered driveway at Christmastime and arriving in their carriages for magical candle-lit Christmas gatherings would become the stuff of legend.

Thanks to their private coal mines, the ready availability of vegetables grown in the kitchen garden and produce from the farms that the Grimshawes owned in the vicinity, the estate was virtually self-sufficient. There was a swimming pool, a private chapel, a tennis court and a school, set up by the family for the children of the workers on the estate. Thanks to their benevolence, the Grimshawes were much respected and their memory lives on to this day in the many tales handed down through the generations of families living in the High Peak.

Samuel Grimshawe, the son of the Samuel Grimshawe who had built Errwood Hall, converted to Roman Catholicism in 1851, having been influenced by friends he had made as a student at the University of Oxford. Inspired by his new-found faith, he created a private chapel at the hall and, as we have learned, he also put up much of the money for the construction in Buxton of St Anne's Roman Catholic Church. In rather less altruistic vein, he invested a considerable amount of money into the purchase of an ocean-going yacht called the *Mariquita*.

The family cruised far and wide in their beloved yacht and soon fell into the habit of bringing back exotic shrubs from their travels, which they would plant in the extensive grounds of the hall. The results of their acquisitions are still clearly visible today, particularly in June when the riotous growth of rhododendrons and azaleas comes into full flower. Visitors now come from far and wide to see this colourful annual display.

As well as returning from their travels with plant collections, the family brought back with them some people they had met on their excursions and offered them employment

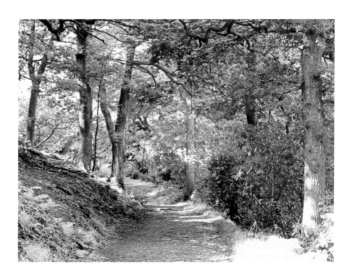

Driveway to Errwood Hall.

at the hall. Ignatious Oyarzabal, who had come from Spain on board the *Mariquita* in 1871, eventually became the family's butler, and his wife, Bridgett, would help in due course at the school that the Grimshawes had set up.

The first teacher at the school was the grandly named Dona Maria Dolores de Ybarguen, a Spanish lady reputed to be of aristocratic descent, who had come to Errwood Hall in 1883 to act as a companion to the second Samuel Grimshawe's widow, Jessica. 'Miss Dolores' was much loved, not only by her pupils but also by members of the Grimshawe family. Sadly, she died, while only in her forties, during a visit to Lourdes.

It is thought that it was Miss Dolores who instigated the building of the shrine that stands on a remote hillside in the fields beyond the hall. The shrine, which is still in a good state of repair, looks rather like a French *borie*, because it takes the form of a circular stone building with a conical stone roof. A mosaic within the beehive-like structure shows St Joseph holding the infant Jesus.

The private burial ground of the Grimshawes is located in fields much closer to the ruins of Errwood Hall. This little hilltop cemetery is a particularly poignant reminder of a family that was such a dominant presence in the Goyt Valley for 100 years. (Readers wishing to learn more about the Grimshawe family are directed to various publications by Gerald Hancock, including *The Goyt Valley and its People.*)

The path that leads back from the hall to the car park on the shores of Errwood Reservoir takes in an extensive view of the man-made lake in its setting of wild moorland and planted forest. Together with recreational opportunities created by the Errwood Sailing Club and the many options for walks on the numerous footpaths, the wonderful combination of wild and tamed landscape elements has made the upper Goyt Valley one of the most popular places to visit in the Peak District. As a result, the road from the Errwood Reservoir car park to the Derbyshire Bridge car park, which stands at the head of the valley, has been made into a one-way street, with vehicular access being barred completely on Sundays and bank holidays from May to the end of September.

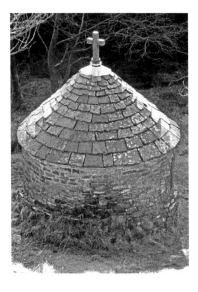

St Joseph's Chapel.

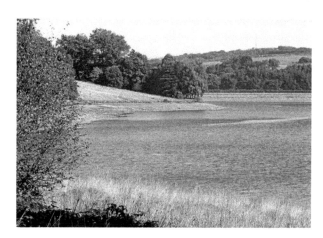

Errwood Reservoir.

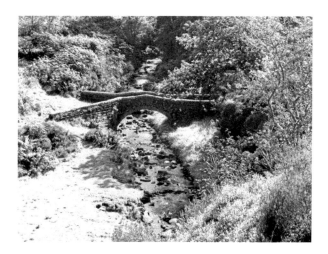

Packhorse Bridge.

To the left of this stretch of road, the infant River Goyt flows under the packhorse bridge that was rebuilt here when the reservoir was constructed. To the right of the road there is clear evidence of a former quarry. In the seventeenth century teams of up to fifty packhorses would transport slabs of stone from the quarry to the surrounding districts and return with their panniers filled with necessary goods for the people living in the valley. It is said that this operation, which was overseen by Thomas Pickford, marked the beginning of the famous removal firm of Pickford's. Who would have thought that a company that is now known nationwide had its origins in a hidden valley in the Peak District hills?

The source of the River Goyt is close to the famous Cat & Fiddle Inn, which is the second highest inn in England at 515 metres above sea level (Tan Hill Inn in the Yorkshire Dales is a few feet higher). The inn, built in 1813, stands in splendid isolation at the summit of the A537, commonly known as the 'Cat and Fiddle road', which links Buxton and Macclesfield via a tortuous route across high, barren moorland. When the travel writer H. V. Morton travelled to the Peak District along this road, he called it 'this wild thing at the very heart of the north country'.

DID YOU KNOW?

The name 'Cat and Fiddle' is said by some to have its origins in the French term *le chat fidéle* ('the faithful cat') but is said by others to be a reference to Catherine Fidele (Catherine of Aragon). As well as the Cat & Fiddle Inn in the Peak District, there are inns that share the same name in Hampshire and Dorset.

This challenging road is even more popular with motorcyclists seeking to test their driving skills than Long Hill, the seventh most dangerous road in Britain where we began our journey. According to statistics compiled by the Road Safety Foundation, we are ending our discovery trail on a road that is more dangerous than any other route in the country.

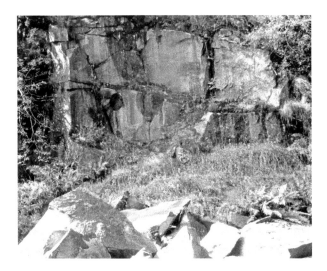

Former quarry.

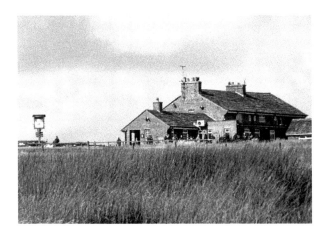

The Cat & Fiddle Inn.

7. Hidden Halls and Hamlets

One of the Peak District's best-kept secrets is that it actually has very few real peaks. There are plenty of edges, ridges and high plateaux in the area, but the number of hills that possess the conical shape of a genuine peak is really quite small. Given this absence, it might be thought that those hills that do deserve to be called peaks would be given due prominence in tourist literature and in the many books that have been written about the area, but Eccles Pike, one of the most shapely summits in the Peak District, is hardly known outside its immediate locality, where it is a much-cherished beauty spot.

Projecting from the centre of a large upland bowl, Eccles Pike is located 2.4 kilometres from the ancient market town of Chapel-en-le-Frith. On its summit there is a 'topograph', deliberately fashioned in bronze to match the pink hue of the unique 'Crist' stone of the area. The topograph is 6 metres in circumference and is engraved with depictions of all the features that can be seen in the fabulous 360-degree view obtained from this wonderful vantage point.

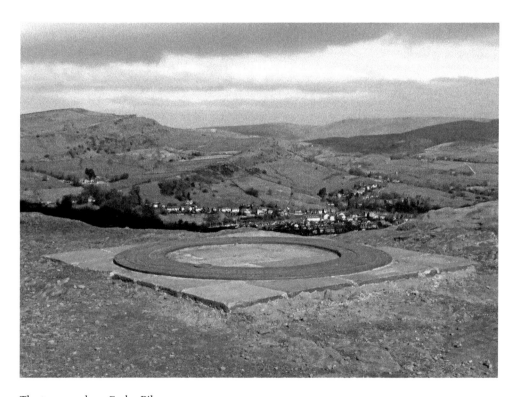

The topograph on Eccles Pike.

Most of the southern horizon is defined by Combs Moss, a 492-metre-high ridge that marks the boundary between the Dark Peak and the White Peak. The valley at the foot of the ridge is occupied by Combs Lake, a reservoir constructed in 1794 to service the Peak Forest Canal, a waterway that carried limestone from the quarries of Derbyshire to the industrial towns of Lancashire. The sailing craft that glide on the shimmering surface of the reservoir look like toy boats when viewed from the Pike, and the grounds of Chapel-en-le-Frith Golf Club on the southern shore of the reservoir look uncannily like the smooth, undulating landscape of Tuscany.

The view to the west takes in Axe Edge, the last great summit of northern England, whereas much of the northern horizon is occupied by the tilted strata of Cracken Edge and the bulky outline of Chinley Churn. Prominent summits on the eastern horizon include South Head, the most shapely of all the hills on the rim of the vast Kinder Scout plateau. A long, sloping ridge runs from the summit of the Pike to the market town of Chapel-en-le-Frith, which was founded in 1225 and built around a chapel in the medieval Royal Forest of the Peak – a 'chapel-in-the-forest'.

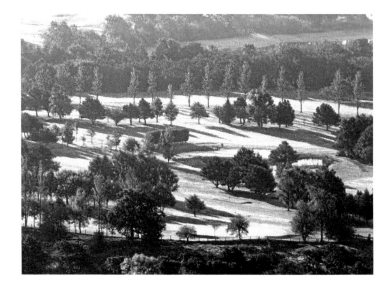

Chapel Golf Course
from Eccles Pike.

DID YOU KNOW?

At sunrise on May Day, the Chapel-en-le-Frith morris men begin a series of dances on the summit of Eccles Pike. The dances they perform are meant to represent a fertility rite. When the morris men performed the same dances in a farmer's barren field on another occasion, no crops began to grow as a result of their efforts. However, a bull escaped during their performance and went on the rampage with cows in a neighbouring field!

While all these features are clearly visible from the summit of Eccles Pike, two other very important elements in the landscape are well hidden. These are the 'secret' hamlets and halls that are tucked into the folds of the dark green hills that form a ring around the Pike.

There have been estates in the parish of Chapel-en-le-Frith ever since they were granted to local families in the fourteenth century in return for the help given to the Crown. Although some of the solid stone halls that stand in these estates have changed hands by purchase and most have been altered over the years, they remain romantic places. Many local people have tales to tell about the halls and their inhabitants.

It is commonly, but wrongly, believed that Judge John Bradshaw, the judge who condemned Charles I to the scaffold in 1649, lived at Bradshaw Hall, a grand house located in a secluded hollow on the southern slopes of Eccles Pike. In fact, the hall was built for the

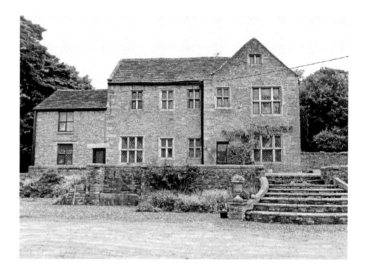

Bradshaw Hall.

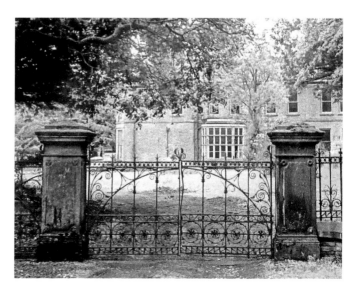

Bank Hall.

judge's cousin, Francis Bradshawe, whose coat of arms adorns the Jacobean gateway of the residence. With its mullioned and transom windows, its array of gables and its cladding of warm brown stone, Bradshaw Hall looks like a sudden vision of the Cotswolds in the heart of the Dark Peak hills. It is one of the most beautiful houses in the Peak District.

A hall with a markedly different appearance occupies a spectacular site 1.6 kilometres to the south of Bradshaw Hall. This is Bank Hall, which stands on the slopes of the high ridge of Combs Moss. The present appearance of the house is largely the result of a Victorian rebuild. In the 1870s, a dining room was added by W. E. Nesfield, a partner of the celebrated architect Norman Shaw. Unfortunately, the extensive panel paintings in this room were sold some years ago, but the delicate stained-glass floral designs on one of the large bay windows have survived.

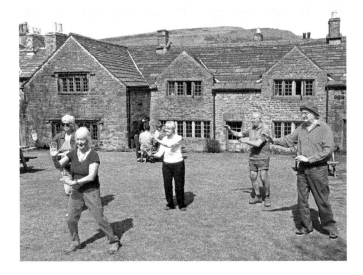

In the grounds of Whitehough Old Hall.

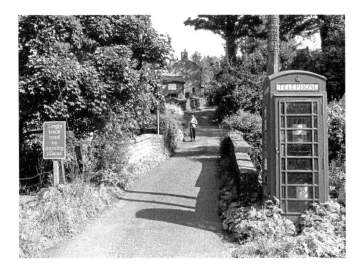

The Wash.

The most famous past resident of Bank Hall is Samuel Frith, known to all as Squire Frith, a Georgian country gentleman, Justice of the Peace, Deputy Lieutenant and High Sheriff of Derbyshire and a fanatical huntsman. The story of a chase that took place in 1788, when a poor fox was pursued relentlessly for 40 miles, is told in Squire Frith's Hunting song, which ends with the lines: 'In a full flowing bowl we will drink a health all, to that great and true sportsman, Squire Frith of Bank Hall.'

Bank Hall stands above the village of Combs, which occupies an idyllic spot between Combs Moss and the eastern shore of Combs Reservoir. A local verse sings the praises of this attractive hamlet in the following terms: 'They rave about the glories of Buxton, In lines that would fill many tomes. Of the charms and beauties of Dovedale, But give me the valley of Combs.' It is even recorded that one resident of Chapel, located just 2.4 kilometres away, was in the habit of taking his annual holidays in Combs.

Another very attractive hamlet is to be found below the northern slopes of Eccles Pike. This is Whitehough, a collection of old cottages and inns, which are gathered around its old hall and situated in a deep, cosy hollow sheltered by the bulk of Chinley Churn. A small monument, adjacent to the village well, carries the inscription '*Pax Vobiscum*', meaning 'May Peace be with You' – an appropriate sentiment in this peaceful little place.

DID YOU KNOW?

A plaque on a rock below the summit of Eccles Pike is a memorial to Highley Sugden, a great benefactor and supporter of the National Trust, the organisation that owns the hill and maintains it for the enjoyment of visitors and locals. Until the final weeks of his long life (he died at the age of ninety-four), Highley could be seen every day, come rain or come shine, walking with the aid of his two Nordic walking sticks to the summit of Eccles Pike.

Long, low and multi-gabled, the Old Hall is said to date from Elizabethan times, although it might be slightly later. A fine minstrel's gallery is a notable feature in one of the rooms that is used as a dining area in the building, which is now a very popular pub and restaurant.

The Wash, a small hamlet a couple of miles east of Whitehough, is another settlement that is tucked into a valley and is sheltered by the surrounding High Peak hills. Its simple stone cottages are set around a meandering stream, but the most prominent building in the village is a former Quaker meeting house. A Quaker burial ground is located some distance away, close to the entrance to the Chestnut Centre, an otter and owl sanctuary, which is set in the grounds of Ford Hall, yet another historic High Peak country house.

Ford Hall occupies a deep valley below South Head, a peak that looks as shapely as Eccles Pike when viewed from certain locations. Nikolaus Pevsner called the Hall a 'mixtum compositum'; it has a mullioned seventeenth-century portion, a Georgian wing, some nineteenth-century extensions and twentieth-century neo-Georgian additions.

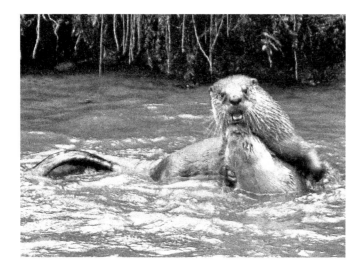

Otters at the Chestnut
Centre.

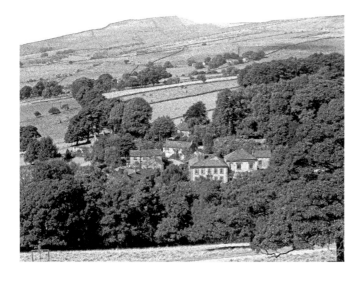

Ford Hall.

Ford Hall is the ancestral home of the Bagshawe family, whose most famous member is
William Bagshawe, widely known as the Apostle of the Peak. William lost his ministry at
Glossop in 1662, when he refused to conform to the Book of Common Prayer. Undeterred,
he continued to hold secret services throughout the High Peak, many of which were based
at Ford Hall.

The beautiful seventeenth-century Independent chapel at nearby Chinley is evidence
of the strength of nonconformist feeling in the area. The building is well hidden, not
so much in this instance by the surrounding hills, but by two curving Victorian railway
viaducts that almost envelope the chapel. The chapel is the final resting place of Grace
Murray, who would have married John Wesley, the founder of Methodism, but for the
objections to their proposed union voiced by Wesley's brother Charles.

Slack Hall (now called Slack Hall Farm), located just outside the grounds of Ford Hall, dates from 1727. This neat, symmetrical, twin-gabled house was the home of the Lingards, who were devout Quakers – several family members are buried in the adjacent Quaker cemetery. The hall stands almost in the path of the main road from Chapel-en-le-Frith to Castleton. This is because the cross-Pennine Turnpike was constructed right through the garden of the hall. When this intrusion occurred, the family decided to vacate their house and move to the new Slack Hall, constructed deep in the valley to the south of the road.

Another ancient hall that is tucked away in the folds of the Dark Peak hills is Bagshaw Hall. This fine house was the residence of the Bagshaws (also known as Bagshawes) before they moved in 1600 to nearby Ford Hall. The house was purchased in 1988 by Martin Street, the chairman of Street Crane, a company that is based in Chapel-en-le-Frith

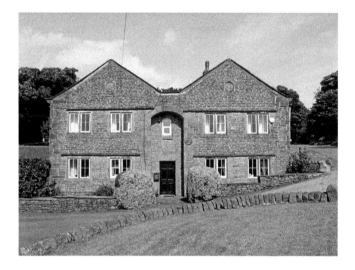

Slack Hall Farm.

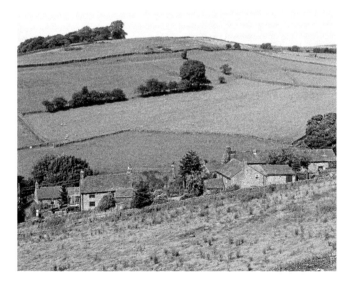

Bagshaw.

and manufactures electrically operated overhead travelling cranes and hoists, many of which are exported to countries throughout the world.

The hamlet of Bagshaw was described in a conservation area assessment carried out for the Peak District National Park Authority as 'sitting within the landscape, following the fall of the land along its length, with individual buildings set either side of a sinuous road'. The secluded settlement has no pubs or shops, no road markings, no pavements and no street furniture, with the single exception of a solitary street lamp.

Some Bagshaw families have farmed the area for many generations, and the hamlet can be traced back to 1251, when it was a settlement in the Royal Forest of the Peak and was recorded as 'Baggesswaes', meaning 'badgers' wood'.

This particular part of the Royal Forest of the Peak, a hunting reserve for the Norman kings, was known as Bowden. The present Bowden Hall was constructed in 1844. In the grounds of the hall, there is a much older stable block, which still carries the arms of the Bowdens. According to William Braylesford Bunting, the author of the standard history of Chapel-en-le-Frith, James Hibberson, who owned the hall in the eighteenth century, constructed a highway through his land in order to avoid having to make a payment at a toll bar on the turnpike.

DID YOU KNOW?

Bowden Hall has been used as a location in two notable productions for BBC television. It featured as a very eerie presence in the supernatural thriller *The Secret of Crickley Hall* and it was also used in a multi-episode production called *The Village*.

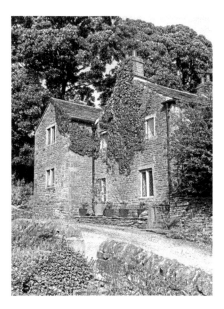

Bagshaw Hall.

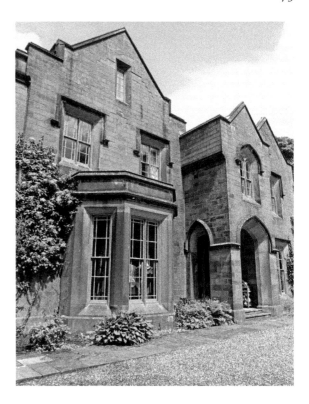

Bowden Hall.

The nearby hamlet of Blackbrook is yet another hidden Dark Peak settlement, comprising just seven households set around a cul-de-sac lane in a wooded hollow. Owned by Michael de Buxton during the reign of Edward I, the Blackbrook Estate passed through several families before much of it was sold off in lots by the Partington family in the 1930s.

The most prominent building in the little hamlet is Blackbrook House, a seventeenth-century property that was acquired by Thomas Partington in 1841 and later refronted in Derbyshire Georgian style. The grounds contain a huge copper beech tree, described by Bryan McGee, the current owner of the house, as having 'a gnarled and twisted crown sprouting immense, cascading branches' and as being 'the finest example of a copper beech in the area'.

The moorland road that has given us access to the delightful hidden hamlets and halls of the Dark Peak hills finally emerges in a surprisingly visible fashion at the village of Sparrowpit. Rather than hiding in a hollow like the other villages in the area, this hamlet stands 366 metres above sea level on the watershed of England. It is said that water released from the front of Sparrowpit's cottages ends up in the Irish Sea, while water released from the rear of the buildings drains into the North Sea.

The high-level, single-street village is highly unusual in having almost all its buildings located on one side only of the steep street. Sparrowpit was nominated by Humphrey Pakington, the author of *English Villages and Hamlets*, as one of the most distinctive villages in England. He memorably described the hamlet as 'a mere handful of grey houses, which has a certain picturesqueness as it stands facing the winds of heaven'.

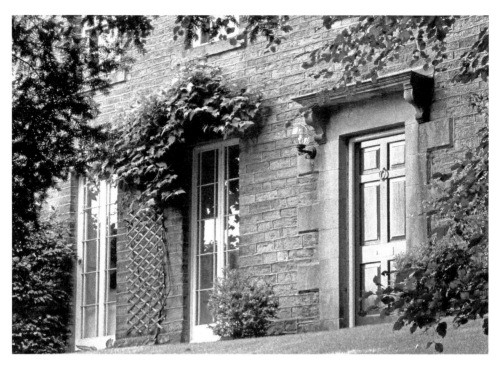

Blackbrook House.

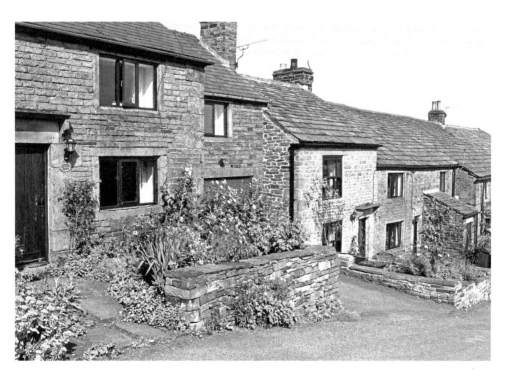

Sparrowpit.

Part Three

The Secret History of Buildings

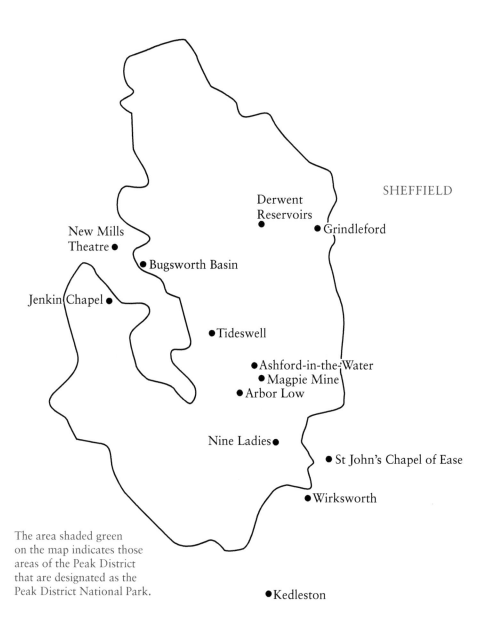

SHEFFIELD

Derwent
Reservoirs
● ●Grindleford

New Mills
Theatre ●
●Bugsworth Basin

Jenkin Chapel ●

●Tideswell

●Ashford-in-the-Water
●Magpie Mine
●Arbor Low

Nine Ladies●

● St John's Chapel of Ease

●Wirksworth

The area shaded green
on the map indicates those
areas of the Peak District
that are designated as the
Peak District National Park.

●Kedleston

8. Two-faced

In and around the Peak District, there are a number of buildings with split personalities. These range from a church that could be mistaken for a castle to a grand country house that possesses two 'fronts', which are equally grand but completely different in style. A building that could easily be mistaken for a country house turns out to be a former cotton mill; four structures that have the appearance of 'medieval keeps' are actually clever disguises for a spectacular example of twentieth-century engineering; and a building with one of the blandest exteriors that one could possibly imagine springs a surprise by having an interior of great splendour.

The church-cum-castle is the Church of St John the Baptist, a small chapel near Matlock Bath. This little-known building is reached by turning off the A6 shortly after the road leaves Matlock and enters Matlock Dale. A steep, narrow side road, known as St John's Lane, winds its way up the western cliff of the dale. After a few metres, there is a glimpse of a building that looks like a fairy-tale castle.

This remarkable edifice is built right up against the side of the cliff. Its battlemented retaining wall is formidably blank and sturdy for much of its considerable height, except for an oriel window that protrudes from the upper reaches. One can easily imagine a beautiful princess being held captive in the room behind this window.

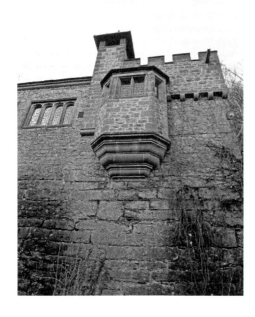

The 'castle wall' of the Church of St John the Baptist.

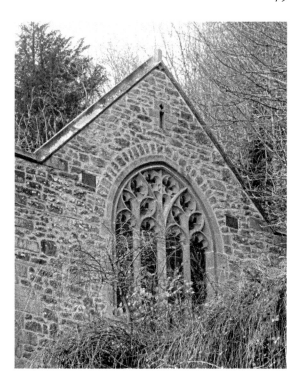

The Gothic window of the Church of
St John the Baptist.

The entrance to the building is reached by continuing up the steep lane for a short distance before turning sharply to the right. A peep through the bars of the perimeter gate brings a complete surprise: the southern façade of the building is clearly not the entrance to a castle at all, but the frontage of a small country church with a picturesque wooden porch and a small bell tower.

This odd little church-cum-castle was designed in 1879 by Sir Guy Dawber, the first president of the Council for the Protection of Rural England, who had been commissioned to provide a private chapel for Mrs Louisa Sophie Harris, who lived in a nearby house called The Rocks. The building is no longer used as a chapel, but it is in the care of a charity known as Friends of Friendless Churches, which has carried out restoration work on this small architectural masterpiece.

Another small chapel with a split personality is the Chapel of St John the Baptist at Saltersford, situated above the Goyt Valley in the western fringes of the Peak District. This little place of worship, commonly known as the 'Jenkin Chapel', stands in an isolated moorland location, close to the intersection of three ancient trackways that were used for the transportation of salt from the Cheshire plain. Although the chapel is located in Cheshire, it stands a short distance from the Derbyshire border and is greatly admired by people who are familiar with this remote corner of the Peak District National Park.

Although the chapel was built in 1733 as a place of worship, its tall chimney stack, sash windows and simple proportions made it look much more like a Georgian farmhouse than an ecclesiastical building. From both the north and south elevations, this domestic appearance is still very apparent, even though the building was made to

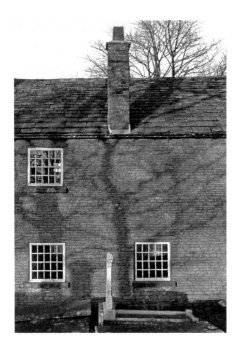

The Jenkin Chapel, looking like a Georgian farmhouse.

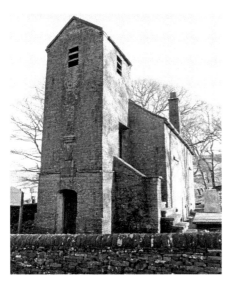

The saddleback tower of the Jenkin Chapel.

look rather more like a chapel by the addition, in 1755, of a simple saddleback tower, which was given an external staircase and a bell chamber.

Although the Jenkin Chapel has a modest exterior, its interior does have a west gallery, an oak pulpit and a reader's desk. Despite the remote location of the chapel, services are held here at 3 p.m. on the second and fourth Sundays in the months between Easter and Christmas.

DID YOU KNOW?

There has been much speculation about the identity of the man who gave his name to the Jenkin Chapel. It has been suggested that he was a trader who sold his wares at the junction where the chapel stands. Another theory has it that Jenkin was a fiery Welsh preacher who delivered sermons at the horse fairs held in the vicinity. A third explanation is that Jenkin was the name of a local family that contributed to the cost of building the little chapel.

A much grander building with a split personality is Kedleston Hall, which is located in a large country estate south of Ashbourne, several miles south of the Peak District National Park. Members of the Curzon family have lived on the estate since the thirteenth century, but the present hall dates from 1758. It was designed in the first instance by Matthew Brettingham and James Paine, two architects who were heavily influenced by the work of Andrea Palladio, who had taken his architectural inspiration from the temples of ancient Greece.

The long north front of Kedleston is pure Palladian in that it relies on symmetry and simple proportions rather than over-the-top decoration. It looks out on to an ornamental bridge, designed as an 'eye-catcher' by Robert Adam in the early years of his career. The work of the young architect certainly caught the eye of Sir Nathaniel Curzon, who decided that he would be happy to allow Adam to take over the completion of the house, the construction of which had got off to such a brilliant start at the hands of Brettingham and Paine.

Adam was wise enough not to tamper with the splendid Palladian north front, but he decided that he would put his own stamp on a new south front, where he ignored Palladian principles and concocted an elaborate façade closely based on the Arch of Constantine in Rome. Thanks to the addition of this spectacular second front, Kedleston became the most impressive two-fronted great house in Derbyshire.

DID YOU KNOW?

It has been claimed that the architect Charles Wyatt copied the design of Kedleston Hall when he built Raj Bhavan in Kolkata (Calcutta), as the residence of the Governor General of India. By a happy coincidence, George Nathaniel Curzon of Kedleston Hall became the occupant of Raj Bhavan when he served as Viceroy of India from 1899–1905.

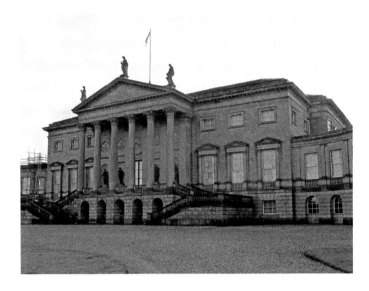

The north front of
Kedleston Hall.

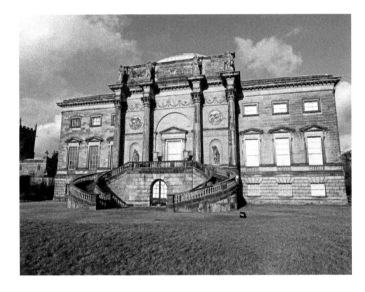

The south front of
Kedleston Hall.

Just visible beyond the four gigantic statues that decorate the frieze on the south façade, there is a tantalising glimpse of the great dome which covers the Salon: a room that ranks alongside the Marble Hall as one of the highlights of an interior that is every bit as wonderful as the exterior.

Another Derbyshire building with an exterior that resembles that of a great eighteenth-century country house is to be found in Cressbrook Dale, where the waters of the River Wye provided the power for some of the country's first cotton mills. This grand building is actually a former cotton mill, rather than a country house.

The first cotton mill in Cressbrook Dale was built for Richard Arkwright in 1783. After this factory burnt down in 1785, it was rebuilt by Arkwright's son, Richard Arkwright II. In 1814

Francis Philips, a Manchester cotton spinner, began the construction of yet another mill in the same location, and it is Philips' mill that has the appearance of a country house. The factory's wide twelve-bay façade has an impressive central pediment, which is topped by a lantern positioned on a hipped roof. However, the interior design was anything but retro in style because it was constructed with cast-iron columns designed to prevent the spread of fire.

The mill closed in 1965, but it has now been superbly converted into apartments, whose occupants enjoy the delights of living in the beautiful valley of the River Wye, where nature has once again replaced industry.

The Wye flows on through delightful scenery to Bakewell, where the first hint of the town comes in the form of a long line of cottages on the bank of the river. Interrupted by several projections and outbuildings, the row of cottages looks very irregular, but these first impressions are misleading. Visitors who enter the town over its famous five-arched, fourteenth-century bridge quickly realise that the irregular row of cottages visible from the river is actually the rear of a prim and very regular terrace of Georgian dwellings on Castle Street.

Bakewell is the chief town in the Peak District National Park, which was designated as England's first national park in 1951. Half a century before the Peak District was given the protection afforded by its status as a national park, one of the valleys in the heart of the region had been flooded to create reservoirs designed to supply the cities of Sheffield, Derby, Nottingham and Leicester.

In an apparent attempt to make amends for the submerging of a previously unspoilt valley, the builders of the reservoirs tried to create new scenic additions to the landscape. These took the form of four massive 'keeps', complete with battlements and

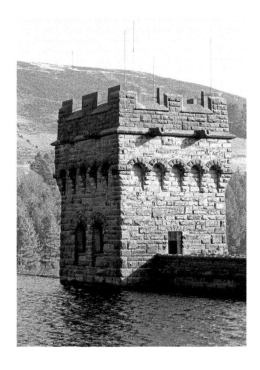

One of the 'keeps' of the Derwent Reservoir.

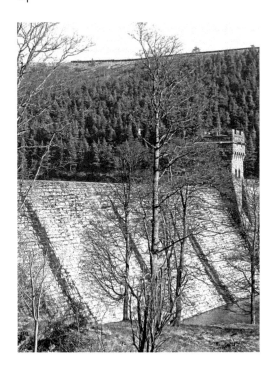

The dam retaining wall.

machicolations, which were positioned on the summits of the retaining walls of the two huge reservoirs that were constructed in the upper reaches of the Derwent Valley.

The wonderful engineering feat involved in the building of the dams is clearly evident to anyone who views the reservoirs from below the massive retaining walls. However, the construction was cleverly disguised as a neo-Gothic fantasy, much as London's Tower Bridge was given a mock-medieval appearance.

The dam project involved over 1,000 workers, who were housed in a temporary 'tin township' known as Birchinlee. Construction of the four keeps and the huge retaining walls required massive blocks of stone being transported on a purpose-built railway from the quarries at Grindleford. One of the keeps now houses a museum dedicated to members of 617 Squadron, who famously used the dams as a training area when practising for their raid on the Ruhr Dams in the Second World War.

DID YOU KNOW?

Birchinlee, popularly known as the 'Tin Town', was built as a temporary township for the families of the construction workers who built the dams in the Upper Derwent Valley between 1902 and 1916. One of the tin huts salvaged from Birchinlee now serves as a beauty and hairdresseing salon in the village of Hope and it has been designated as a listed building.

The two castellated reservoirs in the Upper Derwent Valley were joined by a third reservoir when Ladybower Reservoir was completed in 1945. To allow for this addition, the village of Derwent was submerged and Derwent Hall was demolished. However, the fine oak panelling in the hall was salvaged and inserted into the Mayor's Chamber in the new Council House that was being built at that time in Derby.

Even though the traditional interior of the Derby Council Offices has been completely transformed by a refashioning of the interior to allow 2,000 office staff to be fitted into a building designed for 500, the panelling in the Mayor's Chamber (originally from Derwent Hall) has been preserved. When architect Mike Lampard was asked to come up with a scheme to get a quart into a pint pot, he came up with a design for open-plan office spaces on three levels and a central council chamber that looks like a flying saucer that has landed from outer space. The result is a stunning refashioning of inner space.

This internal transformation is no less spectacular than that which has taken place in a bland-looking building tucked away in the back streets of New Mills. Although this building could easily be dismissed on first sight as a factory or a warehouse, it has a very different purpose, for it is the venue for superb annual productions staged by New Mills Amateur Dramatic and Operatic Society (NMADOS).

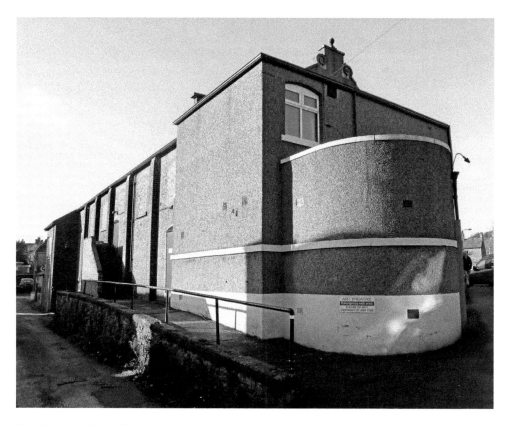

The theatre in New Mills.

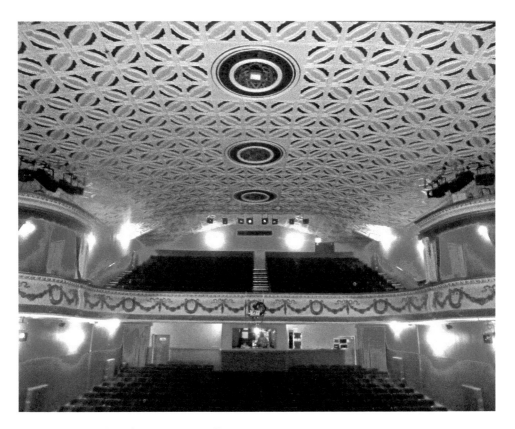

The auditorium of the theatre in New Mills.

The society almost lost their home in the late fifties with the demise of the Art Cinema, which had been based in the building. In desperation, NMADOS took out a temporary lease in the first instance and then raised sufficient funds to buy the place outright. Over the years the society has transformed the interior of this building into a wonderful 500-seat auditorium. The stalls and the balcony are covered by a spectacular ceiling, superbly decorated by Claire Ferriby, who was also responsible for the designs that were added to the interior of the Palace Theatre in Manchester. The large stage, complete with a revolving section, enables NMADOS to put on annual plays, pantomimes and hugely ambitious musicals. Who would have thought that such events could take place in a building whose external appearance gives absolutely no hint of the magic within?

The lesson from this architectural tour of the Peak District is that a building should never be judged on its first appearance. What might look like a castle at first sight could turn out to be a church or even a dam wall; what appears to be a country house might actually be a factory; and a dull exterior might disguise a fabulous interior.

9. Reminders of Times Past

One of the delights of travelling through the Peak District is to come across countless reminders and traces of times past.

Apart from various simple tools and weapons found in caves and rock shelters, very few marks have been left on the landscape by people who lived in the Peak District during the Mesolithic period (8000 BC–4500 BC). However, the imprint left by people living in the area during the Neolithic Age (4500 BC–2200 BC) is plain for all to see, especially at the great stone circle of Arbor Low, situated 373 metres above sea level on the limestone plateau of the White Peak.

Despite, or perhaps because of, the solitude and the eerie silence of this isolated monument, Arbor Low seems to be full of ghostly echoes of long-forgotten rituals. Its spooky atmosphere is captured to perfection in a painting by the Sheffield artist

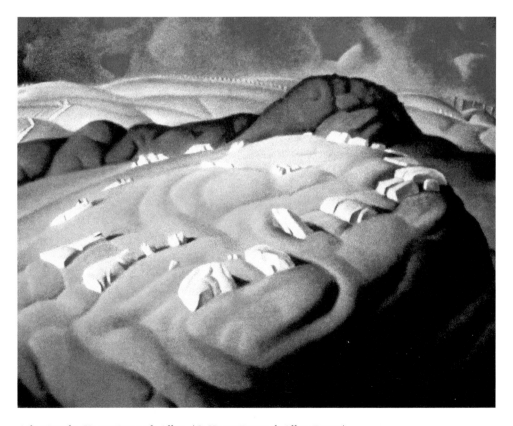

Arbor Low by Harry Epworth Allen. (© Harry Epworth Allen Estate)

Harry Epworth Allen, whose picture shows a line of limestone boulders arranged on the circumference of a large circle on the summit of a prominent mound. In Allen's painting, the limestone boulders seem to emit an unearthly white light that contrasts with the darkness of the mysterious earth hillocks that lie just outside the ring of the henge.

The circular area is 76 metres in diameter and has an inner sanctuary at its centre. It is not known whether the boulders on its circumference were upright when they were first placed here, but all of the large stones now lie flat on the ground, unlike those at other stone circles such as Stonehenge. Some historians have conjectured that the boulders may have been flattened by early Christians in an attempt to de-sanctify the henge. However, it is not even clear whether Arbor Low was actually used as a place of worship. The true nature of the events that took place at the henge remain tantalisingly elusive.

A second Neolithic henge of similar shape and dimensions is situated some 16 kilometres away in the village of Dove Holes, near Buxton. All the stones in this second monument, known as the Bull Ring, have disappeared, leaving a circular earthwork as the only surviving evidence of the stone circle. However, one account, penned in 1789, claimed that a solitary stone was still in existence at that time.

One possible explanation for the disappearance of the stones is that they were utilised as lintels on cottages built in the area. It has also been suggested that any stone fragments that did remain were used as sleepers when the Peak Forest Tramway was constructed in the eighteenth century.

There are lots of standing stones on Stanton Moor, which has been called one of the best-preserved prehistoric landscapes in Britain. The area has no fewer than seventy round barrows and it has a stone circle called the Nine Ladies. This particular henge dates from the Bronze Age, when the fashion was for much smaller stone circles than those that had been constructed in the Neolithic period. The Nine Ladies are accompanied by a 'King Stone', which is situated some 40 metres away.

In the absence of hard evidence about the purpose of the Nine Ladies, it would be tempting to believe a local fable that the circle is actually the result of nine ladies being

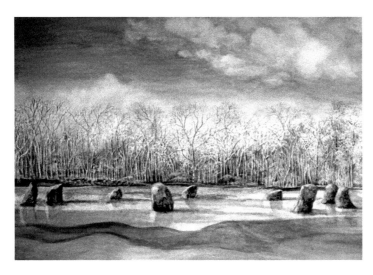

The Nine Ladies by Sue Lewis-Blake.

turned to stone as a penance for dancing on the Sabbath. A painting by Sue Lewis-Blake, who lives in the nearby village of Stanton in Peak, captures the romantic atmosphere of the Nine Ladies in the same way that Harry Epworth Allen's painting captures the mystery of Arbor Low.

Another structure that occupies a commanding position on the limestone plateau is the Magpie Mine, a former lead mine that was worked, on and off, for almost 300 years. This is one of the most memorable sights in the Peak District, but also one of the most incongruous, because the tall engine house and the free-standing round chimney look uncannily like the remnants of a Cornish tin mine.

The appearance of the engine house and chimney is a visual clue that suggests that Cornish miners must have been employed here. In fact, records show that twenty Cornish miners did travel to the Peak District to work in this Derbyshire lead mine in the 1840s.

The gaunt surface buildings of the mine are carefully maintained by the Peak District Mines Historical Society, which also uses the site as a field study centre. An interpretation panel reveals that the engine house and chimney were erected in the nineteenth century, when a Cornish beam engine was installed. The steel headgear and the cage both date from the 1950s, when there was a brief attempt to rework the mine, which had not been operational since 1924.

A metal grid covers the main shaft, comprising a 222-metre vertical drop, with the final 49 metres being under water. When the sun shines through the grilles, it is possible to catch an awesome glimpse of the water far below, and the enormous depth of the shaft

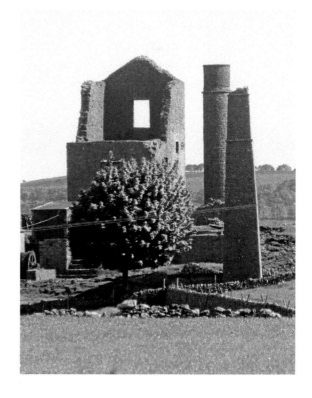

The Magpie Mine.

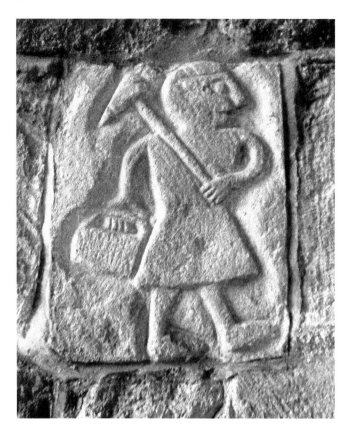

T'Owd Man.

can be confirmed by the inordinate length of time it takes for a small stone to fall from the grid to the surface of the water.

The hardy men who worked at these great depths were always ready to battle with rival miners for the right to exploit newly discovered lead veins. In 1833 the Magpie miners broke through to a vein that was being worked by miners from the Red Soil Mine. Both sets of miners lit fires of straw and tar in an attempt to smoke out their rivals, but the sulphurous fumes created by the Magpie miners resulted in the tragic deaths of three of their opponents. It is said that the widows of the men put a curse on the Magpie Mine that remains in place to this day.

Many of the workers at the Magpie Mine lived in the nearby village of Sheldon, which clings to the edge of the plateau, some 460 metres from the engine house. Although the little settlement can be reached directly from the mine by a footpath, access by road is by a more circuitous route that runs past Johnson Lane Farm and finally enters the village by turning through a right angle near Rose Farm. At the head of the village, which is 305 metres above sea level, there is a large green with a small standing stone, not dissimilar to one of those found on Stanton Moor.

The closure of the Magpie Mine in the 1950s ended the story of lead mining in the Peak District, which began during the Roman occupation of the area. The guardian spirit of lead miners was known as T'Owd Man, whose earliest representation is a carving in

St Mary's Church in Wirksworth. The crude carving shows a miner carrying a pick and a basket known as a 'kibble'.

This carving was originally located in St James' Church in Bonsall, from where it was removed for safe-keeping by churchwarden John Broxup Coates during a major restoration of the church in 1863. When it began to look as if T'Owd Man was in danger of taking up permanent residence in Mr Coates's garden, it was rescued from the churchwarden's clutches and taken to the church in Wirksworth, where it was built very firmly into the wall of the south transept.

Not surprisingly, the people of Bonsall are not best pleased that their carving of T'Owd Man is now in the keeping of Wirksworth Church. However, their pleas that the carving should be restored to its rightful home have fallen on deaf ears, much like the refusal that greeted Melina Mercouri's campaign to have the Parthenon sculptures in the British Museum returned to Athens.

DID YOU KNOW?

Ever since the 1860s, the people of Bonsall have tried to retrieve the carving of T'Owd Man (the Guardian Spirit of Lead Miners) from St Mary's Church in Wirksworth in order to put it in what they see as its rightful place in St James' Church in Bonsall. Their request has been declined and they have had to settle for a replica made by Graham Barfield – a sculptor who lives in Wirksworth of all places!

Representations of a very different kind are to be found on an isolated cottage that stands alongside the road that links the village of Ashford-in-the-Water with the hamlet of Hassop. In the gable of this attractive dwelling there is a delightful visual pun, with depictions of a bell and a gate being used to symbolise a toll bar. As is indicated, the house once served as a toll house, where tolls were collected from travellers using the turnpike that ran alongside the cottage.

Surviving toll houses are found throughout the Peak District, with many of them having become private houses. One of the most distinctive of these is to be found at the entrance to the village of Grindleford. This toll house has a pronounced two-storey, semi-circular bulge designed to allow the toll-house keeper to have an early view of approaching traffic. A toll house in the village of Stoney Middleton provided a similar early view simply by jutting out into the carriageway. Rather than becoming a private house, the Stoney Middleton toll house is now the village chip shop.

The first stretch of toll road in England was introduced on a part of the Great North Road in 1663. This was a result of the passing of an Act of Parliament that allowed tolls to be collected and used to improve road surfaces. In the first instance, the upkeep of the nation's highways was left in the hands of local people, who were required by the Statute Labour Law of 1555 to work on road maintenance for six days each year.

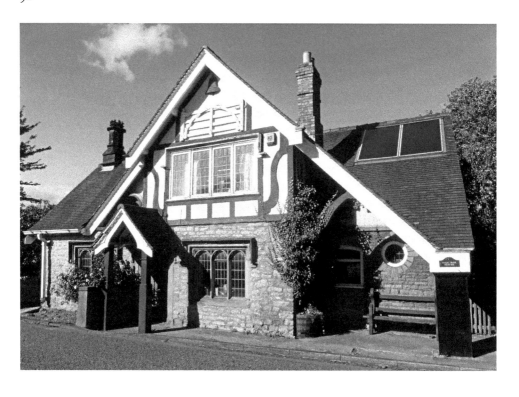

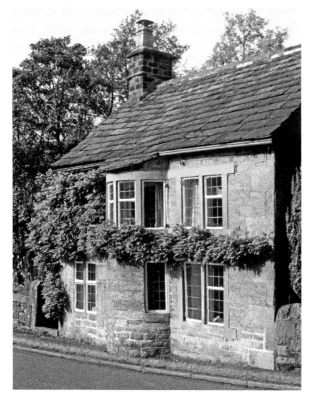

Above: A bell and a gate depicted on a toll house.

Left: The toll house at Grindleford.

By the early eighteenth century it became obvious that Statute Labour alone could not possibly bring about the vast improvement in communications required by the revolutionary changes taking place in agriculture and industry. Between 1720 and 1730, no fewer than seventy Turnpike Acts were passed to allow trusts to collect tolls for the upgrading and maintenance of roads. By 1830 there were almost 1,000 trusts administering 30,000 miles of turnpike roads in England and Wales. Derbyshire had forty separate trusts covering almost 600 miles of road.

The Sheffield–Manchester route over the Pennines was turnpiked in 1758 and its toll bar at Ringinglow, at the entrance to the Peak District moors, proved to be especially profitable. The three-storey, octagonal toll house that was erected at the bar in 1795 still stands and is one of the most distinctive of the many former toll houses that remain in the Peak District.

A second toll house on this route was positioned at Booth Gate above Hathersage. This is a much smaller, single-storey building, but it is equally attractive, because the simple, symmetrical frontage is enhanced by the decorative effect of projecting stone 'kneelers' at the foot of the gable end and by neat dripstones above the door and windows. A toll house with precisely these same details stands alongside Slack Hall Farm, near Chapel-en-le-Frith, at the western end of the route over the hills.

The most difficult section of this Pennine route was the climb up Treak Cliff from the Hope Valley to the hills of the High Peak. Until 1767, the 1 in 5 gradient through Winnats Pass was the only route up this cliff. During the ascent, passengers were often asked to climb down from the coach, not only to lighten the load but also to assist in the whipping of the horses, which struggled appallingly when trying to drag the coach up the steep incline. It was not unusual to see horses left for dead at the side of this road and at the side of other steep ascents in various parts of the country.

DID YOU KNOW?

The Quaker John Woolman was so appalled by the cruelty inflicted on the horses that were used to pull coaches on the turnpike network that he refused to travel by coach or to have any of his mail sent by coach.

Mercifully, the Winnats Pass route was replaced in 1767 by a slightly easier new turnpike road that wound its way up Treak Cliff in a series of hairpins. However, this alternative route was always prone to subsidence because of the unstable nature of the hillside. The road was closed completely in 1979.

The use of horse-drawn coaches for long distance travel was replaced in the nineteenth century by the railways, with the first vehicles to travel along railway tracks being horse dawn. The Peak Forest Tramway, constructed in 1797, was one of the first horse-drawn tramways in the country. It linked the quarries at Dove Holes to the canal basin at

Bugsworth, where waggons carrying limestone that had been extracted from the Peak District were unloaded onto the barges that were used to take the stone to industrial centres on the Lancashire plain.

Horses were only used to pull the waggons on the flat stretches of the route, with a unique gravitational railway being employed on a very steep stretch east of Chapel-en-le-Frith. Loaded waggons travelling down the incline were connected by a hemp rope (later replaced by a chain) to the empty waggons that were ascending the incline, allowing the weight of the loaded waggons to pull the empty waggons up the hill.

Shortly after reaching the foot of the incline, the railway reverted to horse power, with the waggons being pulled through the Stodhart Tunnel, which claims to be the second oldest railway tunnel in the country. The entrance to the tunnel can still be seen in the grounds of The Lodge, a care home near Chapel-en-le-Frith. Unfortunately, the exit from the tunnel was obliterated when a new road was built in the area.

The Peak Forest Tramway closed in 1927 and the railway tracks were subsequently removed. However, surviving stone sleepers can be seen along various parts of the former route of the railway, especially where the tramway entered the Bugsworth Canal Basin. Salvaged stone sleepers have been neatly relaid on this final stretch of the old tramway, and a considerable length of the former route has been converted into a Tramway Trail for the use of walkers and horse riders. Interpretation panels have been placed alongside the path to tell the story of this historic transportation route.

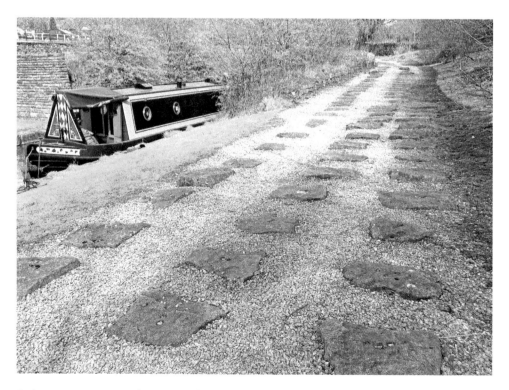

Peak Forest Tramway in the Bugsworth Basin.

DID YOU KNOW?

Braking of wagons on the downward stretches of the Peak Forest Tramway was achieved in a rather alarming way. A brakeman would ride, very precariously, on the edge of the chassis and lock the wheels by leaning over and thrusting a pin into a socket between the spokes.

Further interpretation panels have been erected on the banks of the Bugsworth Basin, which was the largest inland port in the country in its heyday, with 600 tons of lime per day being loaded onto forty barges. Thanks to renovation work carried out by the Inland Waterways Protection Agency, it is now possible for owners of pleasure craft to use the former port as an anchorage after making a journey along the Peak Forest Canal.

The remains of the Peak Forest Tramway and the Bugsworth Basin, the many former toll houses from an earlier era of transportation, the surviving surface structures of the Magpie Mine and the mysterious stone circle of Arbor Low are just a few of the reminders of times past that make a journey through the Peak District so historically fascinating.

Select Bibliography

Christian, Roy, *Derbyshire*, (Batsford: 1978)
Hancock, Gerald, *Goyt Valley and its People*, (self-published: 1996)
Hey, David, *Derbyshire, a History*, (Carnegie Publishing: 2008)
Langham, Mike and Wells, Colin, *Buxton – A Pictorial History*, (Phillimore: 1993)
Millward, R. and Robinson, A., *The Peak District*, (Eyre Methuen: 1975)
Pevsner, Nikolaus, *Derbyshire – Buildings of England*, (Penguin: 1999)
Porter, Lindsey, *Peak District*, (Landmark Publishing: 1998)
Porteous, Crichton, *Derbyshire*, (Robert Hale: 1950)
Redhead, Brian, *The Peak, a Park for all Seasons*, (Guild Publishing: 1989)
Smith, Mike, *Chapel-en-le-Frith Through Time*, (Amberley Publishing updated edition: 2015)
Smith, Roly, *A Peak District Anthology*, (Francis Lincoln Limited: 2012)
Tarn, J. N., *The Peak District National Park – Its Architecture*, (Peak Park Planning Board: 1971)
Thorold, Henry, *Derbyshire – a Shell Guide*, (Faber and Faber: 1972)

Acknowledgements

I am indebted to Joy Hales, editor of *Derbyshire Life and Countryside* magazine, for permission to include some extracts from articles originally written by the author for that publication.

The photographs in the book are by the author, apart from images of the interior of Tideswell Church and Tideswell Well Dressing, used with the kind permission of Bernard O'Sullivan of Inside Out Photography, the photograph of the ceiling of Buxton Opera House (courtesy of Buxton Opera House), reproductions of *Derbyshire Walls* and *Arbor Low* by Harry Epworth Allen (© Harry Epworth Allen Estate), *Nine Ladies Stone Circle* by Sue Lewis-Blake (by permission of the artist), and *The Shrine* by Harry Kingsley (by permission of Buxton Museum and Art Gallery).

I am immensely grateful to my wife Jo-Ann and my daughter Charlotte for all their help and advice during the preparation of this book.